Ancient Greece

Spartans and The Trojan Horse

Table of Contents

Spartans 5

Introduction 6

Copyright Information 8

Chapter 1: The Daily Life of the Spartans 10
   A Brief History of the Spartans 10
   From the Prehistoric Period to the Archaic Period 10
   Classical Sparta 11
   Hellenistic and Roman Sparta 13
   Medieval and Modern Sparta 15
   Structure of Spartan Society 15
   Birth and Death 17
   Women and Marriage 18
   Women's Roles in Spartan Society 20

Chapter 2: Becoming a Spartan Warrior 22
   Spartan Combat Training and Tradition 22
   Spartan Military Tactical Techniques 26
   Pushing 28
   Shields 29
   Hoplite Armament 31
   Deployment into the Battlefield 32
   Stages of Spartan Combat 33

Chapter 3: Battle of Thermopylae 35
   Background on the Battle of Thermopylae 36
   Prelude to the Battle of Thermopylae 39
   Battle of Thermopylae 42
      Day One 42
      Day Two 43
      Day Three 44
   Aftermath of the Battle of Thermopylae 46

Chapter 4: Battle of Plataea 47
    Prelude to the Battle of Plataea 48
    The Battle of Plataea 50
    Aftermath 52

Chapter 5: Battle of the 300 Champions 53

Chapter 6: The Fall of the Spartan Empire 55

Conclusion 59

Bibliography 60

Trojan Horse 62

Introduction 65

Chapter 1: The Bronze Age 67

Chapter 2: Who Were the Trojans 70

Chapter 3: The Mycenaean Greeks 74

Chapter 4: The Prize is Troy 77

Chapter 5: Homer's Reason for the Trojan War 80

Chapter 6: 10-Year War or Many Battles? 84

Chapter 7: Greeks Ready for the Fight 89

Chapter 8: Troy was Safe—At Least in Appearances 93

Chapter 9: Is the Trojan Horse Real? 96

Chapter 10: The Stealthy Greeks 98

Chapter 11: Getting into the City was the Battle 102

Chapter 12: A Horse of a Different Color 105

Chapter 13: The Impact the Trojan Horse Created 108

Chapter 14: The Trojans Lived, Weakened Perhaps 111

Conclusion... *113*
Preview of Greek Gods by Patrick Auerbach............................ *114*

Spartans

The True and Brutal Story of How the Spartans Become the Strongest Warriors in History

Introduction

I want to thank you and congratulate you for downloading the book, *"Spartans: The True and Brutal Story of How the Spartans Become the Strongest Warriors in History"*.

"The Spartans used to ask about the enemy, it was not important how many there are, but where the enemy was" (Plutarch, *Moralia*[1]).

This book contains specific evidence of the steps and strategies on how to live, train, and fight like the Spartans on the battlefield. In addition, this book provides an in-depth examination of the daily lives of the Spartan people in terms of their rituals, gender roles, courtship traditions, as well as some of their leisure activities including javelin tosses. Not only will you be able to learn how to battle like a Spartan, but you may also learn to adopt the simplistic Spartan way of life. Finally, as you progress through the chapters of this book, you will learn the details of some of the most famous battles in Greece fought by the Spartans which led to their rise and fall in terms of authoritative power. Most interestingly is that, through reading this book, you may find some similarities between the political and social actions of the Spartans and the modern-day western views and traditions relating to government. So, strap your feet into your sandals, throw on your finest bronze armor, raise your swords to the sky, and let out your best battle cries as you begin this guided journey through the city-

---

[1] Plutarch, "Apophthegmata Laconica," *Moralia* trans. Frank Cole Babbit, ed. *Moralia* Vol. III Loeb Classical Library, Cambridge: Harvard University Press, 2004

state of Sparta from the prehistoric and Middle Neolithic periods to the classical Sparta period beginning around 480 B.C. as well as the Hellenistic and Roman Sparta periods beginning around 371 B.C. and 146 B.C.

Thanks again for downloading this book, I hope you enjoy it!

Copyright Information

© Copyright 2014 by From Hero To Zero
- All rights reserved.

This document is geared towards providing exact and reliable information in regards to the topic and issue covered. The publication is sold with the idea that the publisher is not required to render accounting, officially permitted, or otherwise, qualified services. If advice is necessary, legal or professional, a practiced individual in the profession should be ordered.

- From a Declaration of Principles which was accepted and approved equally by a Committee of the American Bar Association and a Committee of Publishers and Associations.

In no way is it legal to reproduce, duplicate, or transmit any part of this document in either electronic means or in printed format. Recording of this publication is strictly prohibited and any storage of this document is not allowed unless with written permission from the publisher. All rights reserved.

The information provided herein is stated to be truthful and consistent, in that any liability, in terms of inattention or otherwise, by any usage or abuse of any policies, processes, or directions contained within is the solitary and utter responsibility of the recipient reader. Under no circumstances will any legal responsibility or blame be held against the publisher for any reparation, damages, or monetary loss due to the information herein, either directly or indirectly.

Respective authors own all copyrights not held by the publisher.

The information herein is offered for informational purposes solely, and is universal as so. The presentation of the information is without contract or any type of guarantee assurance.

The trademarks that are used are without any consent, and the publication of the trademark is without permission or backing by the trademark owner. All trademarks and brands within this book are for clarifying purposes only and are the owned by the owners themselves, not affiliated with this document.

Chapter 1:
The Daily Life of the Spartans

A Brief History of the Spartans

"This is Sparta!" (*300*, 2006[2]). Many have quoted this famous line of dialogue from the 2006 blockbuster hit *300*. In fact, over the years, there have been several films based on the history of Sparta. But what exactly was Sparta and who were the Spartans? Sparta was a society located the region of Laconia in ancient Greece that rose to its highest power between 431 and 401 B.C. The people who inhabited to society of Sparta—the Spartans—were a highly loyal militant group, the men receiving intense training for battle when they were only boys and the women, unlike most Greek women at the time, were trained to become intellectual members of society.

From the Prehistoric Period to the Archaic Period

Although the literary evidence regarding events during the prehistoric period of the Spartans is not completely clear, the earliest sound evidence of humans settling within the vicinity of Sparta comes from pottery dating back to the Middle Neolithic period (also known as the "New Stone Age"), found just 1.2 miles southwest of Sparta. Such artifacts are the oldest pieces of evidence of the Mycenaean Spartans, settlers during the final phase of the Bronze Age in Greece, which were

---

[2] *300.* Dir. Zack Snyder. Warner Bros. Legendary Pictures, Virtual Studios, Hollywood Gang Productions, Atmosphere Entertainment MM, Mel's Cite du Cinema, Nimar Studios, 2006

reflected in Homer's *Iliad*. By the end of the Bronze Age, the civilization began to fall due to Macedonian tribes invading Peloponnese, where they were referred to as "Dorians." The Dorians made plans to settle and start a new frontier in Spartan territory, battling the Argive Dorians east and southeast of Sparta as well as the Arcadian Archaeans northwest of Sparta. To date, there has not been any distinct archaeological evidence of the Dorians or the Dorian Spartan civilization along the Eurotas River Valley, where the city of Sparta is located.

The Dark Age of Spartan history is believed to be legendary in that it deals with the Greek mythology, including heroes such as the Heraclids and the Perseids, combining both fictional events and possible historical ones. It is this period of Sparta that provides the first believable sources of Spartan history. From an archaeological standpoint, it is presumed that the first Spartan settlement began around 1000 B.C., two hundred years after the fall of the Mycenaean civilization. It is possible that Sparta's dual kingship government originated from a combining of two Spartan villages during this time period.

Classical Sparta

The Spartans faced a stretch of anarchy and civil conflict during the 7th and 8th centuries B.C. and because of this, a number of political and social policy changes were carried out which the Spartans later linked to the mythological lawmaker, Lycurgus. These changes in Spartan society are used as a starting point for the Classical Sparta period of civilization. During the Second Messenian War, Sparta was established as a local authority in Peloponnese and the remainder of ancient Greece. In the centuries to follow, the Spartans original reputation as a land-fighting people was incomparable to other civilizations in Greece. It is during the Classical Sparta age that the Spartans took part in the famous battles of Thermopylae and the battle of Plataea.

In the latter part of Classical Sparta, Sparta along with Athens, Thebes, and Persia had been the main states battling for dominance over each other in the Peloponnesian War. As an outcome of this war, Sparta became seafaring warriors. Classical Sparta saw the threshold of Spartan power over even the most elite Athenian naval force. As Classical Sparta approached the 5th century B.C., Sparta caught the eyes of many as a society of people who defeated the Athenians overtook Persian territories in Anatolia, marking the period of Sparta's greatest military on land called the Spartan Hegemony.

In the Corinthian War that followed, Sparta was faced with an alliance of the most powerful states in ancient Greece: Thebes, Athens, Corinth, and Argos. This four-way partnership was originally supported by Persia, which had previously been invaded by Sparta in territories within Anatolia and Persians were concerned that the Spartans would expand their invasion further into Asia. Although the Spartans were victorious on land, they did not fare as well on sea as many of their battleships were obliterated during the battle of Cnidus in which Persia provided Athens with a mercenary fleet of Greek-Phoenician warriors. Due to this defeat, Sparta's naval power was severely impaired but the Spartans did not give up their ambitions of invading more territories in Persia until the Athenian general Conon tore apart the Spartan coastline and instilled fear in the Spartans of a rebellion by the helots, state-owned slaves in Sparta.

In 387 B.C., an agreement was set in place called the Peace of Antalcidas which permitted all cities within the state of Ionia in Greece would go back to being under the control of Persia and the Asian border aligning with Persia would no longer be under the control of the Spartans. The outcome of the war was to restate Persia's ability to successfully take part in Greek politics and to reiterate Sparta's declining role in Greek politics. Sparta's rapid decline began after being defeated by the Theban general Epaminondas during the battle of Leuctra, the first land battle lost by the Spartans. Because Spartan citizenship required a blood relation to the original ancestors of Sparta, the enslaved helots began to outnumber the Spartans, leading to the decline of their civilization.

Hellenistic and Roman Sparta

After the battle of Leuctra, Sparta's never completely bounced back from the decline in their citizen population and the revolt of the helots. However, Sparta continued on as a regional authority for the next two centuries. Despite their power, neither the historical icons Philip II or Alexander the Great bothered trying to take over Sparta itself. Going forward, Sparta was often known as the "defender of Hellenism" (Wikipedia[3]) and for its laconic wit even when its population was declining. In an attempt to unify the Greek states against Persian rule, Philip II concocted a league of the Greeks and the Spartans, being the rebels that they were, chose not to participate. The Spartans were not interested in the Greek crusade unless they were able to lead the group. Upon conquering Persia, Alexander the Great, who stood by the league of the Greeks, sent the Athenians three hundred

---

[3] Wikipedia "4th Century BC," *History of Sparta* 5 Mar. 2016. Web. 6 Mar. 2016 https://en.wikipedia.org/wiki/History_of_Sparta#cite_ref-97

Persian armor suits each with an inscription that read "Alexander, son of Philip, and all the Greeks except the Spartans, give these offerings taken from the foreigners who live in Asia" (Wikipedia[4]).

In 333 B.C., during Alexander the Great's reign over eastern Greece, Agis III, the Spartan king at the time, sent a troop of Spartans to Crete in order to maintain a tight grip on the island of Sparta. Then Agis III took hold of allied Greek militant groups. A large Macedonian military led by the general Antipater defeated the Spartan forces in battle, killing more than 5,300 Spartans as well as their allies compared to the 3,500 men who died in Antipater's armed forces. Agis III, who suffered from a combat-related injury, requested that his troops go on without him as he faced the approaching Macedonian military forces in order to buy his troops time to go into hiding. Agis III slayed several rival soldiers before finally being killed on the battlefield. Alexander the Great, displaying a small amount of generosity to the Spartans, only forced them to join the league of Corinth but did not push them to join the rest of the Greeks.

During the Punic Wars, a series of three distinct wars that were fought in Rome, Sparta remained in an alliance with the Roman Republic. The Spartans no longer possessed political independence when forced to join forces with the Archaean League following their loss to other Greek city-states as well as Rome in the Laconian War and the overthrow of Sparta's last king Nabis. One hundred forty-six B.C. saw Greece being taken over by the Roman general Lucius Mummius but the Spartans continued with their own policies and way of life, becoming a

---

[4] Wikipedia "Hellenistic and Roman Sparta," *Sparta* 29 Feb. 2016. Web. 6 Mar. 2016 https://en.wikipedia.org/wiki/Sparta

hot spot for Roman tourists curious to observe the unique customs in Sparta.

Medieval and Modern Sparta

Byzantine sources suggest that certain parts of the Laconian region of Greece remained pagan by nature far into the 10th century A.D. Populations speaking in a Dorian dialect still exist today in Tsakonia, a small region located in eastern Peloponnese. During the Middle Ages, the political and cultural heart of Laconia migrated to the neighboring settlement of Mystras and Sparta's significance in power declined at an even greater rate. In 1834, Sparta was founded once again by a descendant of the Greek king Otto.

Structure of Spartan Society

The Spartan society was constructed as an oligarchy, a governmental design in which power lies within the hands of a select few individuals within the state. Sparta was governed by two hereditary kings from the Agiad and Eurypontid clans, both assumed to be descendants of Heracles (commonly known as Hercules), the Greek mythological god of strength, heroes, sports, athletes, health, agriculture, fertility, trade, oracles, and the divine protector of mankind. The two kings were responsible for overseeing matters of religious, judicial, and military nature. They were deemed the highest priests of the state of Sparta and maintained close contact with the Delphian sanctuary, a separate entity which had always had a hand in Spartan political issues. In 450 B.C., the ruling of the kings were limited to heiresses, adoptions and public roads, described by the famous rhetorician Isocrates (not to be confused with Socrates) as "subject to an oligarchy at home, to a kingship on campaign" (Niebuhr Tod, *The Encyclopædia Britannica*[5]).

A group of individuals known as the ephors (also known as gerousia or "council of elders") took on the state's civil and criminal law cases. The gerousia was the Spartan council of elders consisting of men over the age of sixty and was initiated by the Spartan lawmaker Lycurgus in his Great Rhetra ("Great Proclamation") during the seventh century B.C. This council of elders consisted of twenty-eight men over the age of sixty. Once a man was elected as a member of the ephors, he would remain in the position for life and often he would reside in the home or royalty serving the two kings. The ephor would discuss what modern-day Americans would refer to as "hot button issues" in politics and they would propose alternative solutions to the damos, the masses of Spartan citizens, who would vote for the solution of their choice.

To clarify the term "damos," it is necessary to understand that not all inhabitants of Sparta were classified as citizens. In order to be accepted as a citizen, one must have to pass a Spartan education process known as "agoge" (meaning leading, guidance, and training). All male Spartan men were required to undergo this process with the exception of the first son born to either of the royal families. The agoge process involved stealth training, earning the loyalty of the Spartans, combat training, hunting, dancing, singing, and communication. Usually the only inhabitants of Sparta who were qualified to take on the agoge process were direct descendants of the original inhabitants of the society. Non-

---

[5] Niebuhr Tod, Marcus. "Sparta," *The Encyclopædia Britannica: A Dictionary of Arts, Sciences, Literature and General Information*, Encyclopædia Britannica, Inc., London 1911, 11:611

citizens of Sparta included the perioikoi, who roamed the city freely, and the state-owned slaves known as the helots. Inhabitants of Sparta who were not direct descendants of the original Spartans were not eligible for agoge and Spartans who could not afford the fees associated with the agoge would be in jeopardy of losing their citizenship.

Birth and Death

Because Sparta was a predominantly military state, the Spartan men were often busy training for combat or away in battle and, therefore, they had to enlist a class of slaves called Helots to perform any necessary manual labor within the society. The moment a newborn Spartan was brought into the world, it would almost immediately be trained in physical fitness techniques, especially if the child was a boy.

Not long after birth, a mother would traditionally place her newborn in a tub of wine to analyze its strength. If the child survived the wine bath, it would be brought to the Gerousia by child's father. This council of elders would decide whether the child should continue to be parented. As it noteworthy regarding these birthing rituals, the Spartans were likely one of the first groups of people to have an early method of eugenics. If the council of elders decided that the child was too small or possessed a deformity, it is believed that the child would be tossed into an abyss on Mount Taygetos, known to the Spartans as the Apothetae (a Greek word meaning "Deposits"). While the Spartans are considered to stand out in this respect by some historians, evidence has been acquired supporting that other societies in ancient Greece also practiced discarding children who did not meet the approval of adults. Furthermore, the primitive practice of eugenics in Sparta remains controversial since, to date, only adult bodily remains have been discovered.

Unlike in modern-day western society, a marked headstone on a grave plot was not granted to everyone in Sparta. A marked headstone was earned by soldiers who died in combat during a time of triumph and women who died in service of a sacred institution or during childbirth.

Women and Marriage

As previously stated, Spartan women were unique to ancient Greece in that they were known for being fairly open-minded and were allowed more privileges and power in their society. Women were able to own and manage buildings and were typically free from the burden of domestic duties such as cooking, cleaning, and constructing clothing as these were jobs filled by the Helots. Although the women were not permitted to serve in the military, they did receive an education similar to that of their male counterparts which included studying reading, writing, music, and dancing. However, in order to court men, women often participated in athletic competitions such as javelin-throwing (a javelin is a spear-like shaft that is usually made of wood) or wrestling in addition to singing and dancing contests.

Marriage and procreation were an important part of Spartan life because the council placed pressure on couples to produce male children who could join the ranks of the Spartan military on the battlefield. The Spartans firmly understood the concept of strength in numbers and relied on male children to replace warriors who died in combat. The wedding and marriage customs of the Spartans may seem peculiar to us now, but they were a society with strict traditions and a heavy focus on family. While many ancient cultures would marry girls between the ages of twelve and thirteen years of age, Sparta had a law against young women marrying prior to their early twenties. The rationality behind such a law was to ensure that Spartan women birthed healthy children and to prevent women from experiencing the deathly complications often associated with child rearing before their bodies had been fully developed.

In order to prepare for her wedding day, a Spartan woman would have her head shaved to the scalp by a bridesmaid and would maintain short hair during the extent of her marriage. It is believed by some that the shaving of the woman's head symbolizes her passage into a new stage of life and that the woman was dressed in men's clothing because men, spending most of their lives among other men in the military, were somewhat oblivious to typical expectations regarding a woman's appearance. In addition, the bridesmaid dressed the bride in a cloak and sandals meant for a man and laid her across a mattress in the dark for the groom. The groom, who was to remain sober in order to avoid impotence, would dine with the wedding guests and then slip away to meet his bride and consummate their marriage.

Unlike traditional monogamous couples in the modern western world, married Spartans would live in separate homes since men under the age of thirty were expected to continue inhabiting the military barracks. The only way for men to spend time with their wives during their term of service would be to sneak out of the barracks and return before being caught.

Women's Roles in Spartan Society

Contrary to many ancient cultures around the world, Spartan women possessed great status, power, and were respected citizens of the Sparta society. Beginning from the time that a Spartan woman was born she would hold many of the same rights and privileges as her male counterparts. Young Spartan girls were allowed to exercise, compete in athletic competitions just like young Spartan boys; they were not confined to a future of domestic life as one might expect. The women of Sparta were also highly intelligent in literature and mathematics, which was a rare quality for furthermore, due to the fact that the women of Sparta were restricted from marriage or bearing children before reaching adulthood and that they were well fed and engaged in regular exercise, their bodies maintained in healthier shape and, thus, their life expectancy was longer than that of other Greek women, the average age of death being approximately thirty-five years old.

Although Athenian women wore heavy clothing that hid their bodies from the public eye and were often remained inside their homes, Spartan women draped themselves in dresses with a long slit, which permitted them to move about the city with greater ease either on foot or by chariot.

In addition to their social and intellectual freedoms, the Spartan women exercised economic power since they managed their own properties as well as those of their husbands within the city. Evidence suggests that in the Classical Sparta period, while the male population was falling due to combat-related deaths, women had full ownership of at least thirty-five percent of all property in the city of Sparta, including land. Adding to the Spartan women's socioeconomic power, laws were in place that gave them the same rights as men to divorce.

Despite the Spartans' traditional values of marriage and family, according to visitors of the city, they were also known to engage in "wife sharing," a sort of early form of artificial insemination. With a focus on passing along the genes of the most physically fit Spartans, many older men who struggled with impotency would enlist the assistance of younger more physically fit men to procreate with their wives. Men who had failed to marry or procreate could ask for the permission to impregnate the wife of another man if she had a reputation as a promising child bearer in order to carry on his legacy as a warrior. Because of these procreation practices, Spartan women have often been considered to be polygamous (Greek word meaning "married to multiple spouses"). Due to the Spartans' continuous involvement in battle through their years as a society, this practice was encouraged in order for women to produce many strong children to repopulate Sparta after frequent declines combat-related deaths.

Chapter 2:
Becoming a Spartan Warrior

Spartan Combat Training and Tradition

Many ancient Greek societies such as Athens were heavily focused on visual and performing arts, intellect, and philosophy; however, Sparta was a Mecca for warriors training to shed blood, sweat, and tears in battle. While Spartan women maintained more freedom, the only future for a Spartan man was to live and die with his spear in one hand and his sword in the other.

Once a Spartan by was proven to be physically fit, he faced a future filled with much struggling but if he remained focused on his destiny as a solder, the means would have an honorable end. Spartan boys would spend the first few years of their lives with their parents or their mother and a helot housekeeper but were primed to ponder the military training ahead of them. They would begin their training at the early age of seven years old, when they left home and started the process of Agoge, which was a process that would reiterate the values of Spartan culture. The boys would live under one roof communally where they were divided into groups. While in these training quarters, Spartan boys lived under rigorous conditions, being forced to participate in constant physical competitions involving brutality and violence, offered minimal food portions and were expected to learn a number of combat survival skills including strategies for stealing provisions. The education and training of the boys would be structured with different levels of difficulty based on age, with the first phase of training ranging from six and seven year-olds to seventeen year-olds, then eighteen to twenty year-olds, and after the age of twenty the training would continue until the now men reached the age of twenty-nine or thirty when they were allowed more freedom and rights as citizens.

Teenage boys who showed the most promise on the battlefield and displayed quality leadership skills were chosen to take part in the Crypteia, which was a sort of private police force that maintained a primary goal of antagonizing the general population of helots and killing those who would not follow orders. By the age of twenty years old, Spartan men were deemed full-fledged warriors and would stay on active duty until they reached the age of sixty years old.

In the first phase of their education and training, the Spartan boys would move into their new homes in the military-style barracks with a simplistic look, where they would reside with other boys in their age group. During the second phase, the Spartan boys would become reserve members of the armed forces of the state of Sparta. Although they were not yet classified among the adult male warriors, they would still be enlisted to assist the men on the battlefield in times of dire need. If the boys were not requested to join the troops of soldiers in battle during this phase, they also had the chance to be assigned to a guard as part of the Spartan secret police force. In the third phase of this intense process, when the boys reached the age of twenty years old, the Spartan boys would be accepted into one of many public messes called "syssitia," a type of dining club, through an act of voting, the already existing members of these public messes holding complete power over who is to enter their group. The boys were allowed up to ten years to collaborate with the public messes and earn their acceptance to ensure that they would be voted into the group of their choice.

These public messes each consisted of approximately fifteen members, and each Spartan male citizen was required to join one of them. It was within these public messes that the young Spartan men learned to live as brothers and rely on one another for help when needed. The Spartans were not eligible to become elected members of office until the age of thirty years old. Furthermore, only native Spartans were eligible to become citizens and participate in the training required by law to become warriors of the state of Sparta, and only native Spartans were permitted to join and financially contribute to any of the public messes. Once selected to become a member of an officer's mess, the Spartan man will spend most of the remainder of his life there only to leave from time to time after marriage to fulfill his requirements of a conjugal life.

Sparta is believed to be the first society to ever popularize athletic training in the nude, as the Spartans were confident that the love of an older noble for a teenage boy was necessary to his transformation into a free citizen. The agoge, the education part of a Spartan boy's upbringing, made this aristocratic lover responsible for the boy's training, although this assumption regarding Spartan culture remains in question.

The Spartans' continuous military drills and punishment of the unruly prepared young boys to become skilled at fighting style unique to ancient Greek culture called phalanx formation, a type of combat involving military forces using armor, shields, and long spears. In this phalanx style of combat, the military troop worked as one solid unit, remaining close together and displaying well-coordinated maneuvers in unison. With the exception of the leading general, all soldiers on the battlefield were believed to be equal, lacking specific ranks. Once on the battlefield, an armed solder, which was referred to as a "hoplite," adorned a massive bronze helmet over his head, breastplate armor and ankle guards in addition to a red cloak, and he carried a large round shield constructed from bronze and wood on his arm and he maintained a tight grip on a long wooden spear in his other hand.

Spartan men were pressured to marry at the age of twenty years old but were not permitted to live under the same roof as their wives until they were relieved of their active duty in the armed forces at the age of thirty years old. Despite no longer being an active member of duty at the age of thirty years old, Spartan men still remained as members of the reserve until the age of sixty years old.

While Spartan women were not allowed to participate in military training, they did play a minor role in the cultural rites of passage for men becoming full-time soldiers of the state of Sparta. Thucydides claimed that before a Spartan man left for war, his wife or another significant woman in his life would present him with his shield known as a hoplon and recite the words "With this or upon this," which meant that only a true Spartan would possess the power to return to Sparta either alive with triumphant with their shield still intact on their arm ("with this") or dead ("up this") (Plutarch, *Moralia*[6]). Of course, this traditional phrase was mostly meant to act as political propaganda during war times seeing as the Spartans typically buried their deceased on or near the battle grounds; the remains of fallen soldiers were not carried back to their homes in Sparta. According to Spartan tradition, it was considered less honorable for a Spartan soldier to lose his hoplon than his helmet, breastplate armor, or ankle guards because the hoplon was designed to not only protect him in

---

[6] Plutarch, Frank Cole Babbit, ed., *Moralia Vol. III*, Loeb Classical Library, Cambridge: Harvard University Press, 2004

battle but to also protect the soldier to his left. Therefore, the hoplon was meant to be symbolic of a Spartan soldier's subservience to his fellow brothers in his military unit, his role in the success of his troop, and his dedication to his armed comrades who were often of blood relation.

According to the Greek philosopher Aristotle, the Spartan military ethics were short-sighted and ineffectual. He stated, "It is the standards of civilized men not of beasts that must be kept in mind, for it is good men not beasts who are capable of real courage. Those like the Spartans who concentrate on the one and ignore the other in their education turn men into machines and in devoting themselves to one single aspect of the city's life, end up making them inferior even in that" (Forrest, *A History of Sparta*[7]). Aristotle may have had a valid point, but it is important to bear in mind that he was also known to be a tough critic of Spartan culture and political policies. In addition, there is evidence in existence from the archaic period that suggests that the Spartans were not as narrowly educated as Aristotle assumed, as they also received a thorough education in logic and philosophy.

Spartan Military Tactical Techniques

Similar to other armed forces in ancient Greek city-states, the Spartan armed forces were an infantry-focused organization that battled using the popular phalanx formation. The earliest known display of the phalanx formation of fighting occurred in a Sumerian stone from the 25th century B.C. Although historians are in disagreement regarding the precise relationship between the phalanx formation and the overall

---

[7] Forrest, W.G. *A History of Sparta, 950-192 B.C.*, New York: W. W. Norton & Co. 1968

Greek formation as well as other predecessors of the hoplites, the principles and basic features of the shield wall and spear hedge appear to be universal among all armies incorporating this method of battle. Most historians tend to date the use of the hoplite phalanx formation back to 8th century B.C. ancient Greece in the city-state of Sparta. However, there has been some speculation that the phalanx military tactics could have gone further back to the 7th century B.C. after the introduction of the hoplon in Argos. Another theory regarding the phalanx formation in ancient Greece refers to the possibility that some of the basic techniques used in phalanx formation were apparent in the early years of the Spartans but were still in development due to the still progressing technology.

The hoplite phalanx formation used by Spartans in the Archaic and Classical Sparta time periods (ca. 750-350 B.C.) was a method in which the hoplites would stand in a line in close proximity of one another, their shields interlocking and the first few rows of warriors would launch their spears over the first row of shields. In practicing this strategy, the hoplites would create a wall with their shields to protect them from their enemies with their spears aimed toward their enemies, making it easier for them to avoid being attacked from the front. It also permitted many soldiers to engage in combat simultaneously, side by side.

Most phalanx formation battles occurred on flat solid ground where it was more convenient to remain in a perfect line with fellow soldiers and advance on the battlefield. Land that consisted of hills or rough terrain would make it difficult for the phalanx to maintain in a straight line. Because so many Greek city-states included this method of combat in their war time tactics, they ensured that all battles were initiated on flatlands allowing for a fair fight to the death or—more often than not—a fair fight until one side decided to retreat.

The phalanx formation typically moved forward across the battlefield at a walking pace or a march, although it is likely that they increased their speed in the final few yards of the battle ground to gain momentum against their enemy upon first contact all the while trying not to lose its straight line shape and be rendered ineffective. The Greek historian Herodotus reported that "They [the Spartans] were the first Greeks [at the Battle of Marathon, that] we know of to charge their enemy at a run" (Herodotus, *The History*[8]). Many historians have theorized that the Spartans used this running technique in order to keep their losses from Persian archery to a minimum. With this tactic, both opposing sides would collide into each other which would likely kill a large portion of the front rank of warriors due to the bone crushing caused by the collision. Therefore, the front rank of soldiers tended to have the most vigorous role on the battlefield while the ranks in the back would continue to hold their shields at their chests, pressing them up against the ranks in front for support and protection. When in combat, the entire phalanx formation would move forward in this manner with shields pressed against the row in front of them in an effort to disrupt the perfect formation of the enemy, thus, when contact was made between enemies, it essentially initiated a pushing match.

Pushing

The "physical pushing match" theory is the most widely accredited theory regarding Spartan military combat

---

[8] Herodotus. *The History*, trans. David Grene, Chicago: University of Chicago Press, 1987, 454

techniques (Hanson, *The Western Way of War*[9]). American military historian Victor Davis Hanson has pointed out that it is not easy to account for a solid phalanx formation unless they were used to coordinate the physical act of pushing as explained in the theory seeing as the first couple ranks toward the front would not be able to participate in spear throwing.

Shields

It was customary for each individual Spartan hoplite to bear his shield on his left arm so that he would not only protect himself in battle but he could also protect the soldier to the left of him. Unfortunately, this meant that the soldiers standing to the extreme right were far less protected compared to the rest of the troops and the enemy would often use this weakness to their advantage by attempting to outnumber the right side of the ranks. However, likely to the opposing phalanx's surprise, some groups in ancient Greece such as the Spartans most experienced soldiers were often placed at the far right side of the ranks in the formation to avoid compromise of the phalanx. The downside of this strategy, however, is that now the left side of each rank, which was usually made up of soldiers from allied troops, would now be in a vulnerable situation, thus, it was probably rare that this technique often proved to be successful.

Each row of the phalanx included a leader as well as a rear officer called the ouragos (Greek word meaning "tall leader") who maintained order in the back of the phalanx. The phalanx formation is a prime early example of a military technique in

---

[9] Hanson, Victor Davis. *The Western Way of War: Infantry Battle in Classical Greece*, Berkeley, Los Angeles, and London, University of California Press 1989

which conformity is heavily encouraged for the greater good of the ranks as a whole. Because of the way in which the phalanx formation was designed, the hoplites were forced to trust in their neighboring soldiers for protection and they had to be willing to protect the their neighbors in return, causing the technique to fall in line with the timeless military motto that a troop is only as strong as its weakest link. Therefore, the hoplites' potential for victory in times of war depended on their ability to remain obedient in phalanx formation as well as their physical strength and sense of strong will. The Spartans were also wise in that they typically grouped family and friends close together within the same ranks because they knew that their soldiers would likely make a bigger effort to protect their loved ones than complete strangers and that soldiers who attempted to run and hide would be more likely to be shamed by their peers. More often than not, one side or the other would eventually forfeit and flee the battlefield, allowing their opponent an automatic victory. Ancient Greeks often referred to the word dynamis, which meant the "will to fight," to express the motivation and drive of their warriors.

The Spartan poet Tyrtaeus once wrote, "Now of those, who dare, abiding one beside the other, to advance to the close fray, and the foremost champions, fewer die, and they save the people in the rear; but in men that fear, all excellence is lost. No one could ever in words go through those several ills, which befall a man, if he has been actuated by cowardice. For 'tis grievous to wound in the rear the back of a flying man in a hostile war" (Tyrtæus, *The Idylls*[10]).

---

[10] Tyrtæus, Theocritus, Bion, Moschus. *The Idylls of Theocritus, Bion and Moschus, and the War Songs of Tyrtæus* trans. The Rev. J. Banks, M.A. London: George Bell and Sons, 1878

Hoplite Armament

Each hoplite in the Spartan armed forces was responsible for equipping themselves with their own weapons. The most common weapon used by a hoplite was a spear called a "dory" which was about 7.9 feet in length. It was held in one hand while the other hand carried the hoplite's shield, which was called "Aspis." The head of the spear was typically curved and in the shape of a leaf and the end of the spear contained a spike called a sauroter (meaning "lizard killer") which was used to plant the spear into the ground. In addition, it was used as a secondary weapon in case the main shaft of the spear broke in half or to kill soldiers from the opposing side lying on the ground as their phalanx formation marched forward.

Through the various periods of Spartan history, the armor worn by the hoplites went through a number of changes. During the archaic period, for example, hoplites often wore a bronze breastplate, a bronze helmet complete with cheek plates, and greaves (metal shin guards). However, in the classical Sparta period, the breastplate became less typical dress for soldiers and was replaced with a corselet that was believed to be made of layers of linen fabric pieces that had been glued together or possibly of made of leather scraps sometimes completely or partially covered by with metal scales which overlapped each other. As time went on, the greaves also became less common for Spartan soldiers to be seen wearing and were gradually replaced by heavier armor. This evolution of the armor worn by soldiers was a reflection of the changing times and the attempt to find the balance between being able to move across a battlefield with ease and remaining protection from injury or death.

Deployment into the Battlefield

The composition and strength of a phalanx competition varied depending on the city-state; however, the most basic types of phalanx formation were the stichos (Greek word meaning "file," traditionally consisting of 8-16 men) and the enomotia (Greek word meaning "sworn," traditionally consisting of a maximum of 32 men). Both types of phalanx formations were led by dimoerites who was accompanied by a decadarchos and two decasteroe. Between 4 and 32 enomotiae (depending on the time period and the city-state) would form a lochos (or tactical sub unit of the phalanx formation) led by a lochagos who essentially had command of around 100 hoplites and sometimes up to 500 hoplites during the late Hellenistic period. The Spartans specifically held the standard of "mora," which was the highest standard of hoplitic phalanx formation consisting of 500 to 1500 men led by a general called the strategos. As a whole, the armed forces were ruled by a general's council and the commander-in-chief of the hoplites was called either polemarchos or a strategos autocrator.

Hoplite phalanx usually deployed for combat in groups of 8 or more soldiers deep with the exception of more extreme battle situations such as the Battle of Leuctra which you will read about more in-depth in a later chapter. The depth of the hoplite phalanx formation depended on the need of the armed forces at a given time of war and the plans laid out by the hoplite general.

Stages of Spartan Combat

The following are the five stages of hoplite combat defined:

- *Ephodos*: During this stage, the hoplites cease their singing of their paeanes (Greek word translated as "battle hymns) and advance toward the enemy, gradually increasing their speed and momentum. In the time before impact is made, the soldiers would let out war cries.

- *Krousis*: The opposing phalanx formation make physical contact nearly simultaneously along the front lines of the battlefield. The promachoe (what the Greeks called the front-liners) were expected to not only be physically fit but psychologically fit as well to avoid the potential for second-guessing or wavering decisions in combat. Often times, the men placed in the front row were experienced veterans.

- *Doratismos*: This stage of combat was defined by repeatedly rapid spear thrusting in order to create chaos in the phalanx formation of the enemy. The advantage of using longer spears was that they could successfully separate the opposing formation's hoplites to keep them from assisting the soldiers next to them. This prodding of the opposing formation also worked to leave individual opponents vulnerable to being easily speared. However, it was important that the soldiers did not use their spears to prod too forcefully so that they would not get their spears stuck in shields.

- *Othismus*: Literally meaning "pushing," this stage begins after most soldiers had broken their spears and would begin to shove their enemies with what was left of their spears. This was typically the longest phase of combat.

- *Pararrhexis*: The Greek word meaning "breaching" the enemy, this stage of the basic combat procedure signifies the shattering of the opposing hoplite phalanx formation and the end of the battle. At this time, the cavalry would scatter across the battlefield to pick up the bodies of the fallen soldiers.

Chapter 3:
Battle of Thermopylae

The Battle of Thermopylae was fought by the league of Greek city-states, which was led by King Leonidas of the city-state of Sparta, and the Persian Empire of Xerxes I, lasting a total of three days as part of the second invasion of Greece by Persia. At the same time, the battle at Artemisium was taking place at sea in 480 B.C. The invasion of Greece was a late response by the Persians to the initial failure of their first invasion, which was ended by victorious Athenians during the Battle of Marathon in 490 B.C. Xerxes I prepared for the Battle of Thermopylae by assembling massive naval and army troops as he made plans to conquer Greece.

The Greeks gathered together an armed force of 7,000 warriors who marched north to block the Persians from entering their territory during the summer of 480 B.C. However, it is believed by historians that the Persians greatly outnumbered the Greeks with naval and army troops consisting of approximately 100,000 to 150,000 men strong who appeared at the Greek pass in either August or September of that year. Although the Greeks were outnumbered by the Persians, they were able to keep the Persians at bay for about seven days including the three days of battle before the rear guard of the Greek armed forces was murdered in one of the most well-known last stands in the history of the world. During the first two days of the Battle of Thermopylae, the small group of Greek soldiers were led by King Leonidas to block off the only path available to the Persians to begin an invasion. On the third day, however, a Greek local named Ephialtes was disloyal to the Greeks as he revealed to the Persians that there was a small trail that led behind the Greek border. Aware that his armed forces were being outnumbered sent away many Greek soldiers and stayed to keep watch on their retreat with 300 of the finest Spartans, 700 Thespians, 400 Thebans, and quite possibly a few hundred other Greeks, most of whom died in battle.

Background on the Battle of Thermopylae

Two Greek city-states, Athens and Eretria, had encouraged the failed Ionian Revolt against the Persian Empire ruled by Darius I from 499 to 494 B.C. when the Persian Empire was still developing and vulnerable to revolts against Darius's rulings. As predicted, Darius spent much of his time as king extinguishing the flames of revolt by his subjects. The Ionian Revolt in particular destroyed much of the credibility of his empire and Darius was determined to discipline anyone with any involvement in the revolt, especially the Athenians since he was positive that the Ionians would not get aware with their rebellion without facing the consequences. Ambitious as he was, Darius considered a possible invasion of Greece as an opportunity to stretch his territory further than the borders of the Persian Empire. In order to get the ball rolling on his idea, Darius sent emissaries to all the major Greek city-states in 491 B.C. to request a gift of "earth and water" as a token of their obedience to him. Previously demonstrating the depths of his power just one year prior to this, most Greek city-states voluntarily yielded to this agreement. But the ambassadors in Athens were reluctant to follow suit and were put on trial only to be executed by being thrown into a large pit. The Spartans also refused to go along with Darius and his emissaries and, thus, they were pushed down a well. This signified war between Sparta and the Persian Empire.

In response to the Athenians and the Spartans lack of cooperation, Darius enlisted a task force led by his nephew Artephernes and admiral Datis in 490 B.C., which was instructed to attack Naxos. The task force later moved on to destroy Eretria before returning to Athens at the bay of Marathon and was surprised by the Athenian armed forces. The Athenians saw a great victory at the Battle of Marathon which led the Persian armed forces to run away to Asia.

Learning from his mistakes in the previous invasion attempt, Darius constructs new bigger armed forces troop in order to completely dominate ancient Greece. Unfortunately for Darius, in 486 B.C., his Egyptian subjects began to rebel against him, which delayed his invasion of Greece. Darius soon died while preparing to march into Egypt for a confrontation and the kingship over Persia was passed down to Xerxes I. Continuing the work that Darius started, Xerxes stomped out the revolt in Egypt and proceeded to prepare for an invasion of ancient Greece. Due to the fact that this invasion was meant to be a full-scale one, it was necessary to set long-term goals and plan ahead, store provisions, and enlist as many soldiers as possible to join in this battle. In order to safeguard his territory, Xerxes made the decision to create a bridge over Hellespont, a waterway northwest of Turkey, and that a large hole should be dug along Mount Athos in order for his armed forces to have a way to cross over Europe. Both rather ambitious projects were completed by early 480 B.C. and the armed forces of the Persian Empire began to march toward Europe.

What Darius and the Persians did not know, however, was that the Athenians had also been taking measures to prepare for an invasion of their country since the middle of 480 B.C. and by 482 B.C., the Athenians were working toward building three triremes, or large battleships, necessary for fighting off the

Persians. Unfortunately for the Athenians, they did not have enough men to divide into battles over both land and sea, and this is why the Athenians needed to seek the assistance of other city-states in ancient Greece. While Athenians reached out to their neighboring city-states, the emissaries of the Persian Empire were making their rounds across Greece with the deliberate exclusion of Athens and Sparta. As a result of the Athenians' and Spartans' refusal to support Darius and the Persian Empire, other Greek city-states began to follow suit. A congress of the Greek city-states held a meeting at Corinth toward the end of autumn in 481 B.C. and an alliance between Greek city-states was established. This alliance possessed the power to send envoys to request assistance and to enlist troops from neighboring states to consult with them and stand along the defense lines of battle. Considering how fragmented ancient Greece was at this time, it was a monumental movement for Greek city-states to offer each other support considering the fact that many were still somewhat at war with one another.

This Greek congress met once again during the spring of 480 B.C. and a Thessalian delegate offered the suggestion that the Greeks could gather in Vale of Tempe, a gorge along the borders of Thessaly, giving them the advantage to block Xerxes and his men from invading Greece. An armed force of approximately 10,000 hoplites was deployed to the Vale of Tempe, where they were certain that the Persian Empire's armed forces would be required to pass. Alexander I of Macedon was concerned that the blockage of the vale was not a full-proof plan and that the Persians would find a way to bypass it through Sarantoporo Pass, so the Greek armed forces retreated from this plan. It was not much later that the news spread across the Greek city-states that Xerxes and his army of men had passed through the Hellespont.

In an effort to reevaluate the situation at hand, Themistocles came up with a new strategy for the Greeks to come out victorious. The trail to the southern region of Greece (Boeotia, Attica, and the Peloponnese) would force the Persian army of Xerxes to pass through the very narrow path of Thermopylae. This region could easily be blocked off by the Greek hoplites no matter if they were outnumbered by the Persians. In addition, in order to keep the Persian army from bypassing Thermopylae by crossing the sea, the Athenian navy along with its allies could close off the straits of Artemisium. After much discussion of this plan, it received the seal of approval from the Greek congress and the Greek city-states began working toward executing the plan. However, the cities located within the Peloponnese such as Sparta concentrated on a plan B in order to protect the Isthmus of Corinth in case the battle against the Persians escalated. Meanwhile, the women and children of Athens had been evacuated out of the city-state for safety and sought refuge in the Peloponnese city of Troezen.

Prelude to the Battle of Thermopylae

As the Persian armed forces made their way through ancient Greece, they seemed to be making slow progress as they entered Thrace and Macedon. Unlike the progress made by the Persians, news of their invasion approach traveled fast through the Greek city-states which were due in large part to a Greek spy. During this time, the Spartans armed forces as well as their military leaders were celebrating the festival of Carneia, a celebration which focused on Apollo, and Spartan law stated that there should not be any military activity permitted at the time of such a festival. Thus, the Spartans showed up late to the battlefield during the Battle of Marathon. At this time, the Olympic Games were also taking place, and because of this, it would have been doubly blasphemous for the Spartans to leave for battle during such an occasion. Finally, the ephors that assisted the two kings in leading the Spartans confirmed that the situation at Marathon was too severe and that the Spartan armed forces should deploy at once to assist in blocking the pass under the rule of King Leonidas I. King Leonidas was accompanied by 300 men who served as royal bodyguards and were called the Hippeis. The objective of this mission to Marathon was to gather as many Greek warriors as possible until the arrival of the main Spartan armed forces.

The ancient Greek historian Herodotus reported that the Spartans sought answers from the Oracle of Delphi earlier that year, according to Thermopylae legend:

"O ye men who dwell in the streets of broad Lacedaemon!

Honor the festival of the Carneia!! Otherwise,

Either your glorious town shall be sacked by the children of Perseus,

Or, in exchange, must all through the whole Laconian country

Mourn for the loss of a king, descendant of great Heracles" (Herodotus, *The History*[11]).

According to Herodotus, as the prophecy of the Oracle of Delphi predicted, Leonidas was convinced that he was going to die in battle because he believed that his forces were not capable of a victory, thus, he intentionally enlisted Spartans with living sons so that their legacies would live on should they

---

[11] Herodotus. *The History* trans. George Rawlinson, New York: D. Appleman and Company, 1885, 4:7

die on the battlefield with him. The Spartan armed forces were deployed to Thermopylae from various city-states and consisted of more than 7,000 men by the time that they arrived at their destination. Leonidas elected to set up camp at the "middle gate," which was the narrowest region of Thermopylae and was near a defensive wall that was constructed long ago by the Phocians. Soon after settling at Thermopylae, Leonidas received news from the neighboring city of Trachis that there was a mountain pass that the Persians could use to bypass Thermopylae. In order to resolve the hole in the Greeks' initial plan, Leonidas enlisted 1,000 Phoncians to stand guard atop the mountain to block the Persians from entering.

As the middle of August approached, the Persian army was finally spotted across Malian Gulf on their way toward Thermopylae. With the approach of the Persian armed forces at Thermopylae, the Greeks began their battle cries. A few Peloponnesians, concerned about the potential for victory, proposed a withdrawal from the battlefield to the Isthmus of Corinth, which would block the entry way to Peloponnesus. The neighboring Phocians and Locrians, on the other hand, were determined to defend Thermopylae to the death and request for more assistance. Leonidas kept the peace among the Greek hoplites by standing by them to defend Thermopylae.

The conflict at Thermopylae escalating, Xerxes decided to send an emissary to communicate with Leonidas in the hopes of a compromise. Xerxes offered the Greeks a return to freedom and would deem them the "Friends of the Persian People" in addition to being relocated to better quality land than that which they already owned. However, these offers were denied by Leonidas when he was handed a written negotiation from Xerxes himself which requested that the Greeks forfeit their weapons. Leonidas responded with what has become a famous wise-crack in the history of the world:

Come and take them" (Plutarch, *Moralia*[12]). As the Persian emissary returned to the Persian Empire empty-handed, the progression toward battle was undeniable. Hesitant to take drastic measures, Xerxes waited four days to see if the Greeks would retreat before concluding that a war would begin.

Battle of Thermopylae

Day One

Following the fifth day of the Persians' arrival at Thermopylae in addition to the first official day of battle, Xerxes finally resorted to an attack on the Greeks. First, he demanded that the Persians' five thousand archers launched their arrows but they were unsuccessful when launched from around 100 yards away from their opponents as the arrows seemed to be no match for the Greek hoplites' bronze shields and plate armor. When the attempts with the arrows failed, Xerxes ordered ten thousand Medes and Cissian soldiers to take Greek soldiers as prisoners of war and bring them to him. Next, the Persian armed forces initiated an assault on the Greeks from the front of the line, 10,000 men at a time. The Greeks chose to fight their battles next to the Phocian wall which allowed them to use the services of fewer soldiers than they would have in any other battle. The Greek historian Diodorus reported that "the men stood shoulder to shoulder" and the Greeks were

---

[12] Plutarch, "Apophthegmata Laconica" *Moralia* trans. Frank Cole Babbit, ed. *Moralia* Vol. III Loeb Classical Library, Cambridge: Harvard University Press, 2004

"superior in valor and in the great size of their shields," referring to the phalanx formation strategy popular among ancient Greek military forces (Diodorus, *Diodorus of Sicily*[13]). It was true, in fact, that the Persians possessed weaker shields and smaller spears and swords, which required them to assault the Greeks at a dangerously close range. According to Herodotus, the soldiers from each Greek city-state were kept together as a unit and each unit would take turns entering the battle grounds to participate in combat in order to avoid fatigue of any single unit, which gives an idea of the abundance of the Greek armed forces. Each Greek city-state represented demonstrated somewhat unique battle tactics to their training with the Spartans practicing their classic forging a retreat before performing an about face and annihilating their enemy.

Day Two

On the next day of the Battle of Thermopylae, Xerxes sent in another troop of soldiers to attack the Greeks at the pass, assuming that their enemy was too wounded to continue fighting back. However, as history often tends to repeat itself, the Persian armed forces once again were unsuccessful in their attempted assaults on the Greeks. Frustrated by the failed attempts, Xerxes retreated to his tent on the side lines of the battlefield.

Later on in the same day, Xerxes was contemplating alternative tactics in his tent when he received a piece of good fortune, a Trachinian named Ephialtes told him of a mountain

---

[13] Diodorus Siculus. *Diodorus of Sicily in Twelve Volumes* trans. C. H. Oldfather Vol 4-8 Cambridge, Mass.: Harvard University Press; London: William Heinemann, Ltd. 1989

pass which would allow him to bypass Thermopylae to get to the Greeks. In fact, Ephialtes offered to give Xerxes as well as the Persian army a guided tour of the mountain pass with the hope that he would receive a reward of some kind in return. Since Ephialtes was willing to help the Persian enemy, he went down in history as the ultimate traitor to the Greeks and his name evolved to be synonymous with the Greek word for "nightmare." Herodotus had reported that Xerxes sent Hydarnes, his military commander of the Immortals, to have the Greeks surrounded via the mountain pass without telling Hydarnes who the men were that he wanted surrounded. Hydarnes enlisted 20,000 men to take on this mission.

Day Three

By dawn on the third and final day of the Battle of Thermopylae, the Phocians who were standing guard at the mountain pass took notice of the Persian soldiers arriving by the rustling of leaves. At first, the Persians feared that the Phocians standing guard might be Spartans but Ephialtes assured them that the Phocians were not Spartans. The Phocians ran to a nearby hill to prepare their plan of a counterattack against the Persians. Not wasting any time, the Persians immediately began shooting dozens of arrows in the direction of the Phocians before finally bypassing them to attack the main Greek military force.

Upon receiving the news that the Phocians had not held up the fort at the mountain pass, Leonidas requested a council of war at sunrise. Although some Greek soldiers begged for a withdrawal from the battle, Leonidas insisted on remaining at the pass alongside the Spartans. Many Greek city-states chose to retreat from the battle individually against the orders of Leonidas or were requested to leave the battlefield by Leonidas himself. Despite the vast number of soldiers deciding to flee the battlefield, 700 Thespians who were led by their general Demophilus were determined to continue fighting. In addition, 400 Thebans also chose to stay in battle as well as the Spartans and possibly some Helots.

Although it is often claimed by historians that the Spartans did not retreat from the battlefield due to the laws of Sparta, it is possible that the Spartans earned the reputation of never retreating because of their failure to retreat while at Thermopylae. Furthermore, it is also likely that Leonidas was determined to take his own life for the sake of Sparta as a self-fulfilling prophecy after hearing the words of the Oracle of Delphi.

At sunrise, Xerxes permitted the Immortals enough time to make their way up the mountain pass before advancing toward the Greeks himself. Ten thousand members of the Persian armed forces, which consisted of light infantry as well as cavalry, charged at the front ranks of the Greek phalanx formation. Unlike the last couple days, all of the Greeks now fled from the wall to charge the Persians in an effort to annihilate as many members of the Persian armed forces as possible. When all spears were shattered and broken, the Greek warriors would switch to short swords to kill their enemy. Shot by Persian archers, Leonidas died in combat as predicted in the oracle and both the Persians and the Greeks fought over the king's body lying on the battle ground until the Greeks finally carried him away. Once the Immortals approached, the Greeks retreated behind the Phocian-built wall. As he tore apart a portion of the wall, Xerxes demanded that the hill upon which the wall stood be surrounded by his troops. The pass at Thermopylae now wide open for Persian access, the Persian army was down by approximately 20,000 men.

Aftermath of the Battle of Thermopylae

When Xerxes received word that the Persians discovered the body of Leonidas on the battle ground, he—in a tyrannical state—demanded that the head be removed and the body crucified. This sort of treatment of a corpse was supposedly unlike the Persians, according to Herodotus, as they typically treated fallen warriors with honor and respect. However, Xerxes had a reputation for his uncontrollable rage and, according to legend, it is believed that he ordered Hellespont (yes, a body of water) to be whipped because it would not cooperate with him. After the invasion of Greece had ceased, a stone lion monument was put into place in memory of King Leonidas. The remains of Leonidas, however, were not returned to Sparta and given a proper burial until forty years after the Battle of Thermopylae ended.

It is believed by some that the Battle of Thermopylae was a devastating victory for the Persian Empire since their army appeared to be just as wounded as that of the Greeks. But accounts by Herodotus suggest that this was not the case since the theory ignores the obvious fact that the Persians took over most of Greece and that the Persians continued fighting against the Greeks a year after the battle. One of the most famous moments that took place during the Battle of Thermopylae was that the rear guard stood his ground on the battlefield despite his definite destiny to die in combat.

Chapter 4:
Battle of Plataea

The Battle of Plataea was the last battle fought on land during the second invasion of ancient Greece by Persians. This battle took place during 479 B.C. near the city of Plataea in Boeotia and the conflict lied between the Greek city-states such as Sparta, Athens, Corinth, and Megara and the Persian Empire which was still being led by Xerxes I. During the Battle of Thermopylae just one year prior, the Persian armed forces, led by the then Persian king, had acquired great victories in addition to conquering Thessaly, Boeotia, Euboea, and Attica. However, in the Battle of Salamis which directly followed, the Greek navy alliance came out victorious which protected Peloponnesus from being conquered by the Persians. After this victory by the Greeks, Xerxes retreated along with many of his army soldiers, leaving his general Mardonius behind on the battlefield to finish killing the remainder of the Greek soldiers.

During the summer of 479 B.C., the Greeks mustered a massive army of hoplites and marched out of Peloponnesus. The Persians took refuge in Boeotia and set up a fortified camp site just outside of Plataea. On the other hand, the Greeks avoided being lured into the main cavalry terrain near the Persians' camping grounds, which ended up in a deadlock that went on for eleven days. While plotting a retreat once provision sources were compromised, the Greeks' phalanx formation was disrupted. Assuming the Greeks had already gone into complete retreat, the general Mardonius demanded that the Persian armed forces attack them. Much to the surprise of these Persian troops, the Greeks—mainly the Spartans, Tegeans, and Athenians—stopped and put up a fight, crushing the Persian armed forces and killing Mardonius.

Much of the Persian army soldiers ended up trapped within their camp and annihilated by the Greeks. It was this slaughter as well as that of the Persian naval forces occurring at the same time in the Battle of Mycale which put an end to the invasion of Greece. Following the battles of Plataea and Mycale, the Greek alliance took the offensive stance against the Persians, leading to a new chapter in the Greco-Persian War story. Despite being a resounding victory for the Greeks, the Battle of Plataea seems to carry a different kind of significance compared to the Battle of Marathon in which the Athenians were scored a victory or the Battle of Thermopylae in which the Spartans were sorely defeated.

Prelude to the Battle of Plataea

When the general Mardonius first learned about the Spartan armed forces, he finished destroying Athens by knocking down any building that remained standing. Next, he retreated in the direction of Thebes in hopes of decoying the Greek army into new territory that he believed would be acceptable for the Persian cavalry. Mardonius built an equipped camp settlement on the banks of Asopus River in Boeotia. In response, the Athenians deployed 8,000 men, led by Aristides, as well as 600 Plataean exiles to join forces with the Greek allied army. The army of Athenians and Plataeans marched into Boeotia near Plataea and, under the supervision of commanding General Pausanias, the Greeks lined up opposite the Persians on high ground. Aware that he would be hopeless against the Greeks, Mardonius had to make one of two choices: either disseminate rebellion among the Greek allies or lure them down to the flat land. In addition, Mardonius also acted as an instigator in that he initiated hit-and-run assaults by the Persian cavalry near enemy lines, possibly in attempt to drag the Greeks down to the plain for further attacks. However, the tactic proved unsuccessful when the Persian cavalry commander Masistius was murdered, which became a major deciding factor in the cavalry's plan to retreat.

After the minor victory over the Persians, the Greeks marched onward, staying on higher ground, to a new location better suited for setting up camp as it had a more bountiful water supply. The Spartans and Tegeans stood to the right of the phalanx formation, the Athenians to the left and all other Greek allies on somewhat lower ground in front. To counter the actions of the Greeks, Mardonius led his men to the Asopus and prepared them for battle. Both the Persians and the Greeks, however, refrained from attacking at this time due to bad omens sensed during sacrificial rituals. Both sides remained at their camps for eight days and at this time, the Greeks acquired extra troops. Mardonius was then determined to break the deadlock by ordering his cavalry to initiate an attack on Mount Cithaeron, with the outcome of stolen provisions that were meant to be delivered to the Greeks. With the passing of two more days, the Greeks' provisions continued to be compromised by the Persians. In another menacing attack on the Greeks, the Persians raided the Greeks' supply lines, this time blocking off their water source at Gargaphian Spring. The lack of food and water forced the Greeks to retreat near Plataea where they would have better access to fresh water.

Unfortunately for the Greeks, their retreat did not go according to plan as the allied soldiers in the center of the formation missed their marks and ended up spread out in front of Plataea. The Athenians, Tegeans, and Spartans, who were aligned in the rear of the formation, had not begun their retreat just yet. One division of the Spartan force was, therefore, left behind to protect the back of the formation, retreating further up the hill. Furthermore, the Athenians were ordered by Pausanias to initiate the retreat and meet up with the Spartans. Instead of following instructions, the Athenians at first began to head toward Plataea, further disorganizing the phalanx.

The Battle of Plataea

Once the Persians realized that the Greeks had retreated from their original positions on the hill, Mardonius chose to pursue the Greek armed forces by enlisting an elite Persian infantry, the other Persian troops following behind. By this time, the Spartans and the Tegeans had arrived at the Temple of Demeter. Going against the orders of Pausanias to follow behind the Spartans, the Athenians had been involved with the Theban phalanx formation and, thus, could not assist the Spartans. The Spartans and the Tegeans were the first ranks of the Greek forces to be attacked by the Persian cavalry as the Persian infantry marched forward. After this initial attack, the Persians then laid their shields to rest and began launching arrows toward the Greeks while the cavalry stood back. At this time, the Greek warriors began to duck under the arrows while the Tegeans charged at the Persians' front ranks. Providing one final prayer to the heavens above and a sacrifice near the Temple of Hera, it is believed that the Greeks were finally given good omens and Pausanias ordered the Spartans to continue onward and charge the Persians in line with the Tegeans.

The highest quality Persian infantry was called the sparabara formation; however, it was still no match for the hoplite phalanx formation used by the Greeks. In addition to differing battle tactics, the Persians also used shields made of wicker and short spears compared to the Greeks' bronze shields and longer spears. In an effort to create a fair fight, the Persians attempted to break the Greeks' spears by grabbing them and snapping them in half but the Greeks wisely switched to swords for backup in this situation. Although Mardonius rode in on a white horse across the battlefield with a force of 1,000 Persians guarding him, the Spartans still managed to surround him and hit him directly on his head with a large stone, killing him instantly. With Mardonius no longer around to lead the Persians to victory, many Persian soldiers began to run back to their camp site but his bodyguards stayed behind to fight on his behalf only to be annihilated by the Greeks. Replacing Mardonius for the remainder of the Battle of Plataea, Artabazus, known for commanding the Sieges of Olynthus and Potidea, led 40,000 remaining Persian soldiers away from the battle grounds toward Thessaly in the hopes of eventually reaching the Hellespont.

While the rest of the Greeks continued fighting against the Persians on the other side of the battlefield, the Athenians came out victorious in a rigorous battle against the Thebans. The Thebans ended up retreating in the battle against the Athenians in the opposite direction of the Persians to avoid further defeat. The Greek alliance, now accompanied by the Athenians, invaded the Persian camp site. Initially the Persian forces fought to protect their wall with vigor, but it was eventually compromised as the Persians drew closer and closer together in the camp, ultimately being murdered by the Greeks. It is estimated that after this annihilation by the Greeks, only 3,000 Persian soldiers remained alive of those who retreated.

According to Herodotus, of the approximately 257,000 Persian soldiers who first appeared on the battlefield, it is estimated that only about 43,000 Persian soldiers were left as the battle came to an end. In comparison, the Greeks as a whole are believed to have only lost about 759 soldiers, which include 600 Megarians and Philasians that were annihilated by the Persians' allies, the Theban cavalry. Furthermore, it has been estimated that only 91 Spartans, 16 Tegeans, and 52 Athenians died in combat considering that these three groups were the main forces fighting on the forefront of the battlefield. In total, it has been estimated that between 1,360 and 10,000 Greek casualties occurred during the Battle of Plataea.

Aftermath

The battles of Plataea and Mycale bear great significance in ancient Greek history as the two battles that put a stop to the second Persian invasion of Greece, causing the Greco-Persian War to lean toward the favor of the Greeks. Furthermore, the Greeks stopped the Persians from invading the rest of Europe as well. The battles also signify the superiority of the hoplite weaponry and armor compared to that of the Persian infantry. Going forward, the Persian infantry began enlisting Greek mercenaries because of their well-made materials in times of battle, demonstrating the vulnerability of the Persian forces.

Chapter 5:
Battle of the 300 Champions

The Battle of the 300 Champions, also known as the Battle of the Champions in the time of Herodotus, was fought long after the Battle of Thermopylae and the Battle of Plataea in 546 B.C. between Argos and Sparta. Instead of enlisting the assistance of entire armed forces for this battle, both sides agreed to only recruit their best, most physically fit warriors with the winner of the battle acquiring new territory. The agreement to recruit an equal number of warriors on each side was presumed to serve the purpose of ensuring a fair fight by reducing the potential for a large amount of casualties. In the end, both armed forces marched to their home fronts to avoid the possibility for escalation of the battle.

According to Herodotus, the Spartans had closed in on and seized the plain of Thyrea. While the Argives moved forward to defend the plain, the two opposing armed forces appeared to be perfectly matched so that neither side would be able to one-up the other. The only way to gain victory in this particular battle was to ensure complete annihilation of the opposing side. In addition, it was also agreed between the Argives and the Spartans that member of their troops who became wounded on the battlefield would not be permitted to be taken by the opposing side. A short-lived battle, both the Argives and the Spartans fought against each other until the sun went down and only three men were left on the battle field, two Argive warriors and one Spartan warrior. The two Argives, whose names were Alcenor and Chromius, were at the time confident that they had killed off all of the men in the Spartan armed forces and they had fled the battle grounds to head back to their homes in Argos to celebrate their victory over the

Spartans with the inhabitants of their city-state. However, much to their surprise, they had made one minor error on the battlefield: Orthryades, a wounded member of the Spartan armed forces, had survived the battle. Essentially the last man standing, Orthryades ran home to Sparta to celebrate his supposed victory as well. Orthryades made it all the way to his baggage handlers to tell them of his news and he committed suicide shortly after. Traditionally, Orthryades was not proud to be the last of his troop to survive the battle and it is believed that he took his own life out of survivor's guilt rather than returning to his home in Sparta. Despite this theory for his suicide being in question by some historians, the actions of Orthyrades is significant to the Battle of the 300 Champions because he did not die at the hands of an Argive soldier.

As a result of this misconception by the Argives and the Spartans, both sides of the battle were able to claim to their home fronts that they came out victorious. The Argives were able to claim their victory because, as they initially agreed with the Spartans prior to the beginning of the battle, they left the battle grounds with more survivors. However, the Spartans were also able to claim their victory because it was a Spartan that remained on the field while the two remaining Argives technically fled before the battle could be considered officially over. In the end, the Spartans were the technical winners of the Battle of the 300 Champions and, as a result, they became the new proud owners of the region Thyreatis.

Chapter 6:
The Fall of the Spartan Empire

The city-state of Sparta, which had command of over 3,500 square miles during its classical period, it was one of the greatest military powers at the time. Years after the Battle of the 300 Champions, from 431 to 404 B.C., the Spartans' Peloponnese League took part in the Battle of Mantinea against the democratic power of the imperial Athens' navy forces. The battle lasted longer than either side had originally expected with the Spartan expecting to come out on top with ease. Six years after the initial start of the Battle of Mantinea, in 425 B.C., the Spartan armed forces decided to fake an attack on the region of Pylos on the southwestern Peloponnese coast line, but the Athenian naval troops surprised the Spartans, surrounding them on the island and remind the Spartans that they were not completely indestructible.

More significant to the fall of the Spartan empire, the Athenians' involvement in Pylos during the Battle of Mantinea also inspired the Spartans' government-owned serfs, the Helots, to ponder the possibility of independence and freedom. The Spartans' now feared the potential for a revolt by the Helots which stemmed from manifestation of the Pylos stronghold while the Athenians feared an imperial collapse of their city-state. Although the Spartans and the Athenians agreed to a sort of peace treaty, the Athenians still did not believe that the Spartans could be trusted and began to question their integrity, taking notice of the Spartans secretive ways. With the Athenians eventually surrendering, the Spartans scored a major victory in the battle.

However, thirty-four years after the Battle of Mantinea ended, Sparta was eliminated from the armed forces of Greece, signifying the decline of Spartan power and political influence. There were two kinds of Helots: natives of Laconia and the Messenian Helots, inhabitants of the westernmost point of the Peloponnese who at one point had been free citizens but were taken over by Spartans during the 7th and 8th centuries B.C. The Messenian Helots had not forgotten their former freedom and often acted stubbornly toward their Spartan masters whenever the opportunity arose. During the Battle of Mantinea, many of these Helots fled to the camp site of the Athenians at Pylos, causing the Spartans a mass panic.

Because Spartan society depended so heavily on the manipulation of the Helots for the sake of fulfilling agricultural and other laborious duties as well as gatekeepers during war times, the Spartans enlisted a group called the Similars to keep a watchful eye on the Helots for any signs of a revolt. In fact, to further remind the Helots of their place in the Sparta society, the Spartans would declare war against the Helots every year and individually humiliate them. The Spartans also enlisted a team of assassins who would murder any Helots who acted rebellious in any way, shape, or form at night. As the Spartans began to find more value in the Helots' services, they began to transition the Helots from being butchered at random to recruiting them as mercenaries in battle. However, this makes more apparent an issue that had risen in seriousness by the end of the 5th century B.C.: the declining population of Similars due to war time casualties forced an even heavier reliance on the Helots by the Spartans. Once the Peloponnesian War broke out, Spartan society was wavering and could no longer successfully shield itself from outlying Greek and Mediterranean influence. Thus, the Spartans were deployed far from their home in Sparta, far enough away from the careful observation of their neighbors, and for extended periods of time. As the society of Sparta strived to meet the Athenians' abilities to enlist mercenaries, maintain spread out armed forces for extended periods of time, and assemble a respectable naval force, the Spartan economy greatly expanded which caused fewer opportunities for Spartans to acquire wealth.

Following the Spartan victory in the Battle of Mantinea in 404 B.C., Sparta made alliances as quickly as they broke them with little concern for the consequences as many well-connected members of Spartan society engaged in irresponsible, greedy, and opportunistic military operations and many Spartans found that their home's government did not acknowledge or address such behavior. Other Greeks, whether friends or foes of the Spartans, were no longer impressed by the Spartans and assembled an anti-Spartan coalition. Rapidly losing their diplomatic credibility, the Spartans had no other choice than to attempt to maintain a respected authority through corrupt tactics demonstrated by their armed forces.

The Battle of Coronea in 394 B.C. was a prime example of this. Spartan hoplites were still without a match; however, approximately 350 men were lost, and, thus, victories for Sparta proved to be too costly. Each casualty on the battlefield equaled one less Similar to fight against Sparta's increasingly numerous and driven internal and external enemies. Furthermore, it was no longer evident that Sparta's complete domination of usual hoplite tactics would continue to hold strong. During 390 B.C., the Spartans were shocked by the loss of an secluded Spartan regiment, and a loss of some 250 soldiers by an Athenian force of soldiers and armed, mobile, and incredibly skilled mercenaries who used spears and shields, customary tactics, and weaponry inspired by the mercenary Thracians from the Black Sea shoreline.

Meanwhile, Sparta's rivals were discovering more and more about Sparta's military strategies on the battlefield. It had long been acknowledged wisdom by the Similars that Spartans should avoid fighting the same opponent too frequently. By the time 371 B.C. rolled around, the Thebans had battled the Spartans somewhat continuously for more than two decades and the Theban generals took notice that the Spartans' strengths and weaknesses on the battlefield could be easily exploited to their advantage.

By the Roman era, Sparta had resort to being nothing more than a vacation destination for other Europeans as tourists flocked from around the Greek world to witness Spartan boys suffer through brutal whippings in traditional strength competitions conveniently held in outdoors to accommodate the large crowds of bystanders. These disturbing sources of tourist entertainment stood as unfortunate reminders of the dedication to punishment and public duty that had maintained a formerly proud society of Similar soldiers. Today, the Greek city-state of Sparta is a lively location in the center of Greece with the Eurotas valley in beautiful condition. However, there is little archaeological evidence of the valley's celebrated yet dreadful history. And ironically, the ruins of Messene, where the Helots previously resided, which stand high atop the Kalamata plain, have remained far more remarkable.

Conclusion

Thank you again for downloading this book!

I hope this book was able to help you to gain a deeper understanding of the rise and fall of Spartan society.

The next step is to attempt to relate this knowledge to modern day society.

Finally, if you enjoyed this book, then I'd like to ask you for a favor, would you be kind enough to leave a review for this book on Amazon? It'd be greatly appreciated!

Thank you and good luck!

Bibliography

Diodorus Siculus. *Diodorus of Sicily in Twelve Volumes*, trans. C. H. Oldfather, Vol 4-8, Cambridge, Mass.: Harvard University Press; London: William Heinemann Ltd., 1989

Forrest, W.G. *A History of Sparta, 950-192 B.C.*, New York: W. W. Norton & Company, 1968

Hanson, Victor Davis. *The Western Way of War: Infantry Battle in Classical Greece*, Berkeley, Los Angeles, and London: University of California Press 1989

Herodotus. *The History*, trans. George Rawlinson, New York: D. Appleman and Company, 1885 4:7

Niebuhr Tod, Marcus. "Sparta" *The Encyclopædia Britannica: A Dictionary of Arts, Sciences, Literature and General Information*, Encyclopædia Britannica Inc., London 1911, 11:611

Plutarch. "Apophthegmata Laconica" *Moralia*, trans. Frank Cole Babbit, ed. *Moralia* Vol. III, Loeb Classical Library, Cambridge: Harvard University Press, 2004

Tyrtæus, Theocritus, Bion, Moschus. *The Idylls of Theocritus, Bion, and Moschus, and the War Songs of Tyrtæus*, trans. The Rev. J. Banks, M.A., London: George Bell and Sons 1878

Wikipedia

"4th Century BC," *History of Sparta* 5 Mar. 2016. Web. 6 Mar. 2016
https://en.wikipedia.org/wiki/History_of_Sparta#cite_ref-97

"Hellenistic and Roman Sparta," *Sparta* 29 Feb. 2016. Web. 6 Mar. 2016 https://en.wikipedia.org/wiki/Sparta

300. Dir. Zack Snyder. Warner Bros., Legendary Pictures, Virtual Studios, Hollywood Gang Productions, Atmosphere Entertainment MM, Mel's Cite du Cinema, Nimar Studios 2006

Trojan Horse

How the Greeks Won the Trojan War

© Copyright 2016 by From Hero To Zero
- All rights reserved.

This document is geared towards providing exact and reliable information in regards to the topic and issue covered. The publication is sold with the idea that the publisher is not required to render accounting, officially permitted, or otherwise, qualified services. If advice is necessary, legal or professional, a practiced individual in the profession should be ordered.

- From a Declaration of Principles which was accepted and approved equally by a Committee of the American Bar Association and a Committee of Publishers and Associations.

In no way is it legal to reproduce, duplicate, or transmit any part of this document in either electronic means or in printed format. Recording of this publication is strictly prohibited and any storage of this document is not allowed unless with written permission from the publisher. All rights reserved.

The information provided herein is stated to be truthful and consistent, in that any liability, in terms of inattention or otherwise, by any usage or abuse of any policies, processes, or directions contained within is the solitary and utter responsibility of the recipient reader. Under no circumstances will any legal responsibility or blame be held against the publisher for any reparation, damages, or monetary loss due to the information herein, either directly or indirectly.

Respective authors own all copyrights not held by the publisher.

The information herein is offered for informational purposes solely, and is universal as so. The presentation of the information is without contract or any type of guarantee assurance.

The trademarks that are used are without any consent, and the publication of the trademark is without permission or backing by the trademark owner. All trademarks and brands within this book are for clarifying purposes only and are the owned by the owners themselves, not affiliated with this document.

Introduction

The Trojan War was an epic battle that ended when the Trojan Horse filled with Greeks was received inside the city gates of Troy. This is the summation of what could be history or myth.

According to Homer's Iliad and The Odyssey, the Trojan War was fought because of gods and goddesses, who always liked to play with humans. History tells of something much different. In fact, for several centuries, historians have been trying to prove that Troy actually existed and was not a mythical city.

Until 1871, it was believed the Trojan War was nothing but an epic poem, created by a Greek poet, Homer. It was considered a fictitious account, with no bearing on the real world whatsoever.

Few facts were known prior to 1871, which could be used to determine there was ever such a battle between Greek forces and Trojans protecting their coastal city. It wasn't that war didn't exist or that the Trojans weren't real. It was rather the sparse historical accounts of such an epic war. Plenty of poems and stories based on mythical gods and goddesses were written years after the supposed war, but nothing in the actual history books of the time or since the "Trojan War" lent to the credibility of the story.

Yet, the legend created by Homer continued to plague historians and archeologists. It became a mission for some individuals, including Heinrich Schliemann and Frank Calvert to prove Troy was an actual city that existed in times of antiquity.

Today the question is not about whether Troy existed or did not. It is now fact that there was a city called Troy, where the

Trojans lived, and it was under continued battle against enemy forces.

The real question is—did the Trojan War, as we have come to think of it happen or was it a series of small battles that eventually led to the end of the Trojan people?

Was there, in fact, a Trojan Horse and if so, how did it help win the war for the Greeks?

The focus of the coming chapters, will be to discuss the Trojan Horse as a real concept, not the fictional one from Homer's epic poem. The focus will not be to tell you how Achilles entered the city and helped win the war.

Instead, you will learn who the Trojans were, which Greek faction fought against the Trojans in the last battle, and why the war or series of wars occurred, which led to the innovative concept of the Trojan Horse. In the end, you will also learn the impact the "Trojan Horse" has had on more recent wars. You will discover if the Trojans died out never to be heard of again or if one war ended and more simply occurred.

Chapter 1:
The Bronze Age

Background is needed to answer why the Trojan War occurred and how the Trojan horse was used to win the war. By becoming familiar with the Bronze Age, you can begin to understand the puzzle archeologists are finally starting to uncover.

The Bronze Age is defined by the smelting of copper and tin or by the trading of bronze products. It is also categorized as the third millennium B.C. However, this means different things depending on the regions of the world being discussed.

The Near East, which categorizes the following countries: Anatolia, Elam, Caucasus, Egypt, Mesopotamia, the Levant, and Sistan, were in the Bronze Age from 3300 to 1200 B.C. Later, you should remember that Anatolia was also considered Asia Minor. Anatolia is now called Turkey.

South Asia was said to be in the Bronze Age from 3000 to 1200 B.C. Europe, which includes Aegean began their Bronze Age in 3200 to 600 B.C. Greece was considered as a part of Europe even then, and had a hold on Aegean property, as well as control of the Aegean Sea.

To put these Bronze Age dates into perspective, Greece was a mighty power starting from 1600 B.C. to the end of 1100 B.C.

Note: Many historians trying to prove the existence of Troy, the Trojan War, and the Trojan Horse, believe the Bronze Age ended in 1100 B.C. in Greece and much of the Near East. This will not be debated in this book.

According to the Troia Archeological Site website and UNESCO World Heritage Site, the land considered to be a part of the City of Troy was inhabited from 3000 B.C. to 500 A.D.

The part of this wide range in time period that most concerns us is 1300 to 1000 B.C. It is generally accepted that Homer's Troy and the Troy that fell due to the Greek's Trojan Horse existed sometime between 1300 and 1150 B.C.

Carl Blegen was an archeologist, who worked on the site now considered Troy, between 1932 and 1938. Blegen's chronology of the Troy Strata provides a look at 1300 to 1000 B.C.

Strata is a geological term meaning the layers of earth archeologists have dug up in an attempt to discover historical evidence that will help us understand the ancient civilizations of Troy.

These strata are named by site level: Troy VIh, Troy VIIa, Troy VIIb1, Troy VIIb2, and Troy VIIb3. There is an approximate end date for each site level, meaning the civilization that existed prior to the dates was in some way damaged.

Troy VIh was said to have ended in 1300 B.C. due to an earthquake. Any buildings, people, and artifacts discovered from this time period show a great geological event, such as an earthquake that made people flee and leave everyday items behind.

The next end date for Troy, was 1230-1190/1180 BC, which was Troy VIIa. The listed probably cause was an attack by an enemy. In 1150 BC, Troy VIIb1 was destroyed by an unknown cause. Troy VIIb2 ended in 1100 BC, either due to an earthquake or enemy attack. Troy VIIb3 ended sometime in 1000 BC from an unknown cause.

Troy VIIa is the most important strata. Several archeologists, including Blegen, Schliemann, Calvert, and Strauss accept that the Troy mentioned in the Iliad and Odyssey; therefore, the Troy associated with the war was the Troy VIIa. Blegen has more to support the claim. When digging to the Troy VIIa, he uncovered many unburied skeletons, with Mycenaean Greek arrowheads near the bodies, suggesting the war occurred.

As the discussion deepens about Troy, the Mycenaean Greeks, and the Trojan Horse, remember the probable "Trojan War" was sometime around 1230 to 1180 B.C. This has to do with the unburied skeletons, carbon dating of those skeletons, and the geological evidence that provides a narrowed timeline. The main evidence to suggest this is when the 10 years of war occurred, is a lack of any other cause for the destruction of the city, as well as Homer's account. It also sets a timeline for the information to come in discussing why the war started and how it ended.

Chapter 2:
Who Were the Trojans

Archeologists and historians generally accept that Trojans are a mixture of Anatolian and Luwian origins. This was not always the case. For years, the only evidentiary support that Troy and Trojans existed was Homer's tales. It might seem like the book keeps bringing in Homer and the question of the history versus the myth, but in actuality, to understand the full answer this book is going to provide, you must have a knowledge of the "players."

In Homer's account of the epic war, he used the Greek spelling for names. It seems obvious now that he did so because he was Greek and because when the story was written Greek was a well-known language. To earlier archeologists who were trying to prove the City of Troy existed, there was a 10-year war, and the Greeks won, any information from Homer's epic poems that corresponded to known history was important.

Archeological digs have since answered the question of who the Trojans really were, without any mythological or inaccurate historical assumptions. Archeologists firmly believe the Trojan people were of Anatolian and Luwian decent because of artifacts, buildings, and rituals.

Historical Context Uncovered by Schliemann and Others

Frank Calvert went to what is now Turkey to uncover the true City of Troy. He was not a very well-known archeologist at the time, mostly due to lack of funding and being self-taught. Heinrich Schliemann was largely considered a fraud and discounted for his belief in Troy, but he at least had the funds to make the dig known to the world and to tell the newspapers that he had at last found the real Troy. This occurred in 1871.

What Schliemann considered Troy was little more than a mound of earth, some uncovered bits of pottery, and a deep belief that he was right. Like many in the archeologic and the scientific academia world, proving or discounting a theory is powerful stuff.

Archeologists like Blegen, who arrived in Turkey in 1932, came with the idea of proving Troy existed and uncovered half an acre of the city. It was the citadel. Fast-forward 130 years since Schliemann found his mound, and it is 1988. Strauss and others did their part to uncover a total of 75 acres of city.

In the 1930s, historians postulated that Troy was a mere citadel on the coast of Turkey and not the opulent fortress that the Greeks feared. Yet, 50 years later, with more digging, more strata uncovered, and reaching Troy VIIa, it was known that the city was every bit as large as Homer depicted in his epic tale. It is also at this time, origins of who the Troy descended from were uncovered.

The City Layout, Pottery, and Burials

With the entire city of Troy uncovered by archeologists, work could begin uncovering the Trojans' origins. The city layout represented Anatolian construction. The position of the citadel versus other buildings, including the architecture of those buildings represented the Anatolian culture more so than the Mycenaean Greek culture.

Quite a bit of pottery was uncovered. Again, the majority of the pieces represented an Anatolian connection, where the minority of pieces related more to Greece. Given the shipping lanes for goods coming from Asia through the Aegean Sea and past the strait, where Troy was built, it is not unlikely that traders from Greece sold their pottery in Troy.

Archeological digs uncovered burial grounds, which indicated Anatolian burial practices versus those of the Greeks.

If you add in the location of the city, which was in Anatolia or what is now called Turkey, it would make sense for the Trojans to be descendants of earlier Anatolian people.

There is evidence to suggest a larger Greek population did live in Troy, but this was after the Trojan War is thought to have occurred. This evidence is based on layers of artifacts, in which Greek artifacts were found in strata nearer to the top than Trojan relics.

Where Science Has Yet to Reach

DNA mapping is now possible. More and more species, including human species are being mapped to determine origins. Quite a bit about the skeletons found from prehistoric eras is known thanks to DNA. However, the skeletons found at Troy and thought to have been involved in the Trojan War have yet to undergo DNA profiling, at least that has been released to the public for consumption.

When assessing information for DNA confirmation, it seems scientists have made it as far back as determining the origins of the Etruscans. This is mentioned only to show that the Trojan heritage did not die out completely. DNA evidence shows Etruscan origins relate to the Hittite, and Lydian Kingdoms. Troy was a part of these two kingdoms. More detail about the Hittites will be discussed in chapters about why the Trojan War occurred.

Given the interest in Troy in the academic world, it is likely that DNA profiling of skeletons found at the City of Troy will someday be conducted as a way to answer more questions about the time and the people who lived there.

For now, the simplest answer to who were the Trojans is—Anatolian descendants.

Chapter 3:
The Mycenaean Greeks

In any war there are always at least two parties involved, if not a few other countries because they share alliances with one of the main parties waging war. It might seem a waste of words to discuss who the Greeks were. When discussing the Trojans, there is a question because early assumptions said they were descendants of Greece, when in fact the Trojans displayed more of an Anatolian heritage.

You might even say, "duh they were Greeks." But did you know, there were Mycenaean Greeks and Dorian Greeks living during the Bronze Age? Were you aware that certain cities like Pylos and Athens were populated by Mycenaean Greeks and many of the Dorian Greeks had started to migrate out of Greece, weakening their strong positions as they headed across Europe?

As with many cultures, there are clear divisions, even within a broad term to mean a certain origin. A great example shows that today, labelling someone from Korea as Asian. Yes, Asia as a continent is very large, but it encompasses many cultures, who are diverse in their beliefs, way of life, and language. Chinese is very distinctive from Korean, as is Japanese from the other two languages. Therefore, it is important to know who the Mycenaean Greeks were.

The Mycenaean Period

The Mycenaean period is a time when the Greek mainland was enjoying power and wealth. Their strong holds were Mycenae, Thebes, Tiryns, and Athens. Greek workshops were filled with pottery, bronze, jewelry, carved gems, vases, glass ornaments, and precious metals.

The Mycenaean Greeks had a wide reach for their commerce, sending goods from Greece through the Mediterranean, basically extending from Spain to the Levant. Evidence from this time suggests vases, oil, and wine were the primary goods of trade.

These Greeks were more than traders. They were also warriors and engineers. They created bridges, beehive-shaped tombs, and fortification walls using Cyclopean masonry. The Mycenaean's also established irrigation and drainage systems. Mycenae was viewed as a rich city of gold, while Pylos was sandy (Homer's description). Tablet evidence that were used to record history by scribes, indicated Greece had a very organized feudal system in place. According to Colette Hemingway and Sean Hemingway, the late 1300 century B.C. or 1200s, was a time of decline for the Mycenaean Greeks. The important sites, which had been filled with wealth, suffered destruction, and many Mycenaean's started moving to remote settlements. Pylos, which was the city the king inhabited was destroyed sometime in 1200 B.C. However, it is not completely gone, since it is still a city in Greece and called Pylos-Nestoras today.

Historians consider the complete collapse of the Mycenaean Greeks occurred by the end of 1100 B.C., while many collapses in their cities from 1300 to 1180 B.C. threatened ultimate destruction. It was also a time of rebuilds for parts of the cities the Greeks felt were important.

There is a bit of debate about this time, where some scholars feel it was the population movement that made the Mycenaean's weak. Those who study the Trojan War are more inclined to think it was internal battles, as well as trying to over-stretch their forces to expand and take over cities of shipping importance.

Other Important Players

The world did not consist of just the Trojans and Mycenaean Greeks. There was a lot of strife, natural disasters, and internal wars that started to change existing kingdoms beyond what occurred in Troy and Mycenaean Greek cities.

The Hittites ran a powerful kingdom, which also included Troy. Around the same time Troy fell, Hattusa, the capital of the Hittite Kingdom, was destroyed. Aramaic nomads and Chaldeans were threatening the survival of the Assyrian and Babylonian empires. The Dorian Greeks were migrating and expanding, causing trouble for the Mycenaean Greeks.

It was suggested that the Mycenaean's and Hittites had a peaceful relationship, due to respect and mutual fear of destruction. An accord between Hittite King Hattusili III and King Ahhiyawa of the Mycenaean Greeks existed.

However, Egyptian factions and others like Piyama-Radu constantly moved against the Hittite Kingdom. These two cultures wanted to expand from Africa into Asia, and this was difficult because the Hittite fortress walls were strong. King Ahhiyawa was given Lesbos by Piyama-Radu during the 13th Century B.C. Piyama-Radu even tried to enter Troy as a way to get to the capital of the Hittite Kingdom.

Evidence suggests the relationship with Piyama-Radu was more important to the Greeks than keeping the peace with the Hittite King. Although, for a time after King Hattusili III asked to restore peace, King Ahhiyawa did accept.

Chapter 4:
The Prize is Troy

Examining a map of the world and its countries today, Turkey is north of the Mediterranean Sea. This was Anatolia and during the Trojan War it was a land held by the power of the Hittite Kingdom. Between Greece and Turkey is the Aegean Sea, where the land is split by the Dardanelles, a narrow strait that leads to the Sea of Marmara and then through another strait into the Black Sea. Gaining access to the Black Sea meant trade ships could reach eastern Europe, Russia, and what is now Georgia.

Greece held power in the Mediterranean and Aegean Seas. As a large trade country, with amazing engineering feats, including their ships, it was easy for Greece to control the two seas.

The one thing that stopped Greece from moving east through Asia, was the land on the other side of the Dardanelles, which the citadel of Troy protected.

This land was considered blessed, where water was found in abundance. Clean, drinkable water was imperative and Troy was able to tap into it. The land was also perfect for growing grains and supporting cattle. The seas held plenty of fish to ensure Trojans had plenty of food.

The Trojans were considered middlemen in the shipping industry. The city had little to trade other than textiles and horses. In fact, Troy was known for their exceptionally well bred horses. The city was becoming rich off of controlling travel through the strait and due to the Boreas winds.

For 30 to 60 days in summer the winds would blow making trade easier in the Aegean Sea, through the strait, up the Sea of Marmara and into the Black Sea. When the wind died, ships could not sail because they were not able to tack or go in a zigzag pattern yet.

Ship captains would have to dock at Troy when the winds stopped. It could be for a day or several days that these ships would be moored at Troy. Naturally, it meant trading. Trojans would provide food and lodging to these ships' captains and crew.

Discord over middlemen getting rich was definitely in existence. Greece, of course, wanted the fortress to increase their own riches, as well as to make their way into the Hittite community. Troy was a good place to provide military protection from the west for the Hittite kingdom.

It is clear through various texts, both written history and fictional accounts that Greek perceived Troy as a threat and temptation. Trojans were a threat because they could decide to advance across the strait into Greece and try to sack cities. Troy could also try to take control of the Aegean Sea and become more powerful in the shipping community.

It is clear when examining history, Troy was a prize to win for several opposing forces. Digging through the layers of earth to uncover the history of Troy, it is clear the Trojans faced several skirmishes from the beginning of the Bronze Age till the end of Troy as a city in 500 AD.

It's All About Location and Desire

The predominant theory as to why the Trojan War occurred, either as a 10-year war or several small, intense skirmishes for

10-years, is that Troy was a prized location to the Mycenaean Greeks.

The Greeks desired expansion and control of such a wealthy city. Who needed a middleman getting rich, when it would be better to own the citadel and the city? By owning the city, access to the Hittite Kingdom, Asia Minor and the rest of Asia was easier.

Great leaders and warriors would have thought of this, even as they made living everyday life a priority. The combination of the location of Troy and the desire to be a strong nation that could become richer from controlling the shipping trade would have led to the Mycenaean Greeks developing strategy after strategy to finally sack Troy and end the Trojans.

As the number one reason for why the Trojan War began, was continuously waged, and finally won, was the desire to own the location and make Troy the prize.

Chapter 5:
Homer's Reason for the Trojan War

A battle so epic, it has been recorded in the Iliad, continued in the Odyssey, and written about by different authors for centuries, according to Homer it was started over a woman.

Helen of Troy, a beauty beyond compare, and is said to have started the war between the Mycenaean Greeks and Troy. Helen, according to Homer, was the daughter of Zeus. She was a Greek goddess, wife of Agamemnon, and Prince of Troy's Paris' lover.

The Iliad tells of a diplomatic trip Paris went on to Agamemnon's kingdom in Greece. It is said he was there to bring about a better relationship between Greece and Troy, for trade. In part, many believe he was meant to assure Agamemnon that the Trojans would not rise up against Greece.

The trouble with this tale is that it was an epic poem, written by Homer based on various elements in history, not always taken from 1300 to 1180 B.C. Homer was born centuries after the supposed 10-year Trojan War.

Now we know the Trojan War was at least an event, the debate as to whether it was 10 years in length like the epic battle of Homer's stories or more likely small, intense skirmishes for more than 10 years—is still ongoing.

Scholars of history, archeology, and literature can at least agree that a war or series of wars sacked the city of Troy sometime between 1230 and 1180. More evidence is coming to light in the 1990s and 2000s, suggests the series of battles that eventually ended the Trojans as a people and culture happened between 1200 and 1180 B.C.

We know approximately the when, a general length of the battle, and the where. We also know a bit about the main players, as they were Mycenaean Greeks and Trojans.

Figuring out the direct cause based on literature and what few historical records have been uncovered, is more difficult. Did Helen of Troy actually exist as a real person and not the mythical God, Homer made her out to be? There are no records in Mycenaean Greek or Trojan history that talk of a woman called Helen.

Does this mean she couldn't be real? No, historically women in earlier centuries, including right up until the mid-1900s, were considered an inferior sex. Yes, women could be revered as goddesses, but human females were considered far in-superior to men. If we assume the wife of the current Greek King did exist and she ran off with the Prince of Troy, we could also assume the Greeks were too humiliated at such a wanton act. It can also be assumed that Troy, having ended due to such an act was unable to record the history and just as ashamed of their prince. It is a lot of assuming to do.

A thread of credibility for Homer's Helen of Troy can be found in Hittite records, which mention Akagamunas as the ruler of Ahhiyawa in the 14th century B.C. Based on the spelling and translation into Greek this could refer to Homer's Agamemnon.

Historical Records from Numerous Cultures

There are several cultures nearly from the beginning of the human race that would suggest wars were fought over women.

Kings saw their daughters as sacrifices in marriage to opposing kingdoms. Even in more recent history, the concept of marrying a princess or a royal woman to a prince or king was used to keep peace between two countries. England's history reflects this rather well.

If the princess or royal woman refused, it would be cause for war. It could also be said that the daughter was sent as a peace offering, while a strategy was in place to gain access to the kingdom and take it over with an easier war.

A more relevant concept is the Middle Eastern wars, occurring for the most part due to religious difference. Yes, the "war on terror" is being fought because of 9-11, but there is also a reason relating to "women's rights" and helping women who are suffering or at least not seen to have equal rights. The point is not to debate this current and major fight, but to point out that "women's rights" is bandied about as one reason for military personnel to remain in the Middle East. It gives credibility to the wars being fought with the excuse of a woman or women as the catalyst or a major reason for the fight.

It is very possible that a war could be waged over a woman who ran from her husband to the prince of another country. For now, it is just a theory based primarily on Homer's account of the Trojan War.

If we believe his account as completely, historically accurate, save for the goddess and gods and other mythical elements, then we would need to believe the Trojan War was fought because of one woman's actions and a Trojan prince.

An Excuse to Sack Troy

It is plausible the Mycenaean Greeks used a woman as an excuse to fight the Trojans on their turf. The king of the Mycenaean's could have requested his best warriors take their best ships and start attacking the citadel and attempt to access the city. It would have been a great excuse to fulfil the known desire the Greeks had in wanting Troy and control of the Dardanelles.

The fact that Homer's account makes it a more romantic and tragic tale of a great city coming to its knees in defeat over a woman just makes it a more interesting account of history than the cut and dried version that could have been written.

Will the answer to the question- why did the Trojans fight the Mycenaean Greeks occur and end in defeat for the city of Troy, ever be known? It is unlikely. After 145 years, the answer is still unknown. There are still too many questions and theories being postulated by historians and archeologists because the records are too sparse.

If we assume Homer wrote about a real woman and named her Helen to protect the parties involved centuries later, then we can assume the war's catalyst was this woman.

If we assume there was no woman, then the Greeks found another catalyst to continue pressing the walls of Troy until finally, the Greeks were triumphant over the powerful citadel and the warriors of Troy.

In the end, the reason why the war started is up to you, the reader, to decide knowing both the location as a reason for war and the historical knowledge that women made a great excuse for kings to wage war on other kingdoms.

Chapter 6:
10-Year War or Many Battles?

The Trojan War is considered a ten-year siege on the City of Troy, which ended when the Trojan Horse was rolled into the city, filled with Greeks. However, it may not have been the epic ten-year battle of Homer's epic poems. Does this affect how the war ended—if it was not a ten-year constant siege? Yes, it could definitely affect the validity of the Trojan horse and what was supposedly accomplished with such a Greek creation.

If the validity of Homer's tale is found to be completely false, then it stands to reason, the Trojan horse may be a figment of imagination too. The difficulty historians and archeologists had in believing the Trojan War was actually a real battle comes from the way of life at the time it was said to happen.

There is no doubt that battles occurred with regularity. It doesn't matter whether you look at Egypt, Greece, Troy and the Hittite Kingdom, Ancient China, or any other history of a society and a race of people. War was as common in everyday life as eating.

The basic human instinct to survive, prosper, and find happiness drove societies throughout the known world in the Bronze Age. For a country to survive against another, strength, strategy, and fighting was necessary. It was only the strongest, most prepared who could survive the fights an opponent would start. Fear was certainly a driving force.

Fear that someone else would attack first. Fear of the next opponent being stronger or smarter, or having a better strategy was normal. Women, children, men could not go on with their life each day and think they were totally safe—not like we do today.

When war is half a world away, it is easy to forget that somewhere people are dying in the name of religion, because they made the wrong gesture or said the wrong thing to the wrong, powerful person. In the Bronze Age, it was not possible to forget that death could come during sleep, when awake, or when trying to avoid a fight.

Battles are still continuously waged, even if there is a break in the middle. For a moment consider World War II and Christmas Eve. For one night, both forces, sang and stopped fighting. The next day, the peace was over and fighting began again.

North Korea and South Korea are locked in a battle, where the Demilitarized Zone lay between the border. One country is forever split in two, until something happens to break the tenuous peace.

Already in discussing the Mycenaean Greeks, their relationships and power, as well as that of Troy, you know battles were ongoing. If it was not Egypt trying to break through the Hittite Kingdom and destroy the capital, then it was the Greeks fearing Trojan expansion or vice versa. So there was most certainly war being fought between the Greeks and Trojans, which could have started due to a woman or not.

What one has to figure out is whether that war was non-stop for ten long years or if it was a series of powerful battles that finally ended with the destruction of Troy VIIa.

A Series of Battles is More Likely

As stated, times were hard for those living during the Bronze Age. Unlimited supplies are not something that existed. Travel by ship could take half a year or more because the winds might have stopped for several weeks during the journeys.

Longevity of the people was significantly less due to famine, disease, war, and natural disaster. Population growth, while significant for the time, did not mean there were always enough men to fight a continuous battle.

One small battle, fought with the Trojans sending arrows down into the hearts of Greeks below could have taken out an entire fleet and stopped the war. New warriors would have needed to come to replace the dead, but could Greece spare these warriors to continue the war for ten years?

Greece had other borders, other relationships, and internal struggles to contend with. The reality of the situation is— Greece could not have sustained sending troops year after year, for ten years to try and take over Troy.

It is more likely that attempts were made when Greece felt fear, when a new excuse to fight, or peace in their own land made it possible to try again to end the Trojan society.

That one army, of tens of thousands, continued to attack day in and day out, until the idea of the Trojan horse was formed, is 99% impossible according to most archeologists studying Troy.

Supporting Facts

Back in the chapter about the various strata layers, you learned Troy was destroyed multiple times. Sometimes the city was destroyed because of natural disasters that led to fire and the Trojans abandoning the city, only to come back and build it again.

In between 1300 and ten00 B.C., archeological evidence, is unable to prove a long, never ending war was waged on Troy. The facts show a natural disaster, an attack by an enemy, unknown reasons for destruction, more enemy or natural disaster issues, and more unknown reasons for the city to end.

There is also evidence that sometime between 1200 and 1180, Mycenaean Greeks finally entered the city of Troy, killed numerous Trojans, and left them unburied as they ended a great and powerful city.

The layer of earth on top of this time shows the city was eventually rebuilt, destroyed again and again, with new cities until finally in 500 AD Troy was forever abandoned.

Based on what we know about society and life during 1230 and 1150 B.C. historians can postulate with some accuracy that the siege was a series of battles, with a final brilliant move. The question of whether Troy existed, whether there was at least some type of war, is answered.

Is it like Homer wrote or what many continue to debate as truth—no, not entirely. Proving one theory beyond a reasonable doubt is not possible given the few records that exist about Troy and its end sometime around 1180 B.C.

It would be nice if one opinion or archeological theory proposed by those digging at Troy could be proved true. It would end the debate of what was or could have been. For now, all readers can do, is know that there was war, natural disasters, and Troy were built over and over again, until the city was finally abandoned, forgotten and covered by layers of earth most likely blown around by the Boreas winds so desired by the ship captains of the Bronze Age.

You can choose to believe ten years of constant war occurred each day, until evidence conclusively states otherwise. Ultimately the important point is—the Trojan society written about by Homer was lost. Descendants moved on, a new city was built and new ancestors lived and died on the earth once known to house the grand city of Troy.

Chapter 7:
Greeks Ready for the Fight

The starting point for any information relating to Trojan War is always Homer's sensational epic poem. It might irritate to keep repeating this, but one has to understand to discuss a historical account of the Trojan War, one has to continually refer to the information Homer wrote and any other writers after that. The Aeneid is another tale using the concepts of the Trojan War based on Homer's works. But rather than getting sidetracked on all the books that have been written, it is time to discuss what might have happened during those ten long years in battle.

Assuming it was really ten years, the Greek army had to ready for the battle they would wage from the sea. The Dardanelles strait is 38 miles long and anywhere from 0.75 to 4 miles wide. Today under a mile and up to 4 miles does not seem like a great journey. It can be done in a matter of minutes in the power boats we have today. Ferries, which traverse this area daily do so several times a day.

In antiquity, this was not the case. Greek ships, while advanced, were still under the power of a sail and many men rowing oars in the hold. Historical accounts believe the Bireme, a type of Greek warship, was used in the Trojan War.

It was a long ship, with 30 oars or so on each side, and hundreds of men were needed to power this ship across the sea. The front was shaped in a triangle pattern, with the back turned up to hold the sail in place. It was a longer and narrower ship than the sailboats we are more familiar with today. There was also only one mast, with the sail parallel with the length of the boat, instead of perpendicular.

These ships were made to skim over the water and not to displace a lot of water. In fact, the hulls were flatter than the sail boats that came centuries later. The house had to be flatter, for the ships to move quickly through the water, and even then it could take a great deal of time.

Historical accounts do not state if there was any way from Greece to Troy, other than by ship. While the Greeks did know how to build bridges, there is nothing to suggest they could build an extension bridge about a mile long to go from Greece to what is now Turkey.

Biremes were not made for hauling supplies. They were made for hauling warriors, who had to power the ships across the water. It would have been a tiring prospect. Imagine rowing for days, hoping the wind would help, and eventually reaching Troy.

Only your armada might have been seen or the Trojans could have been expecting it to arrive. Any lookout in the citadel would have known the Greek warships for what they were, since trade ships were much different in shape and size.

Additionally, if the war was started because Paris or whoever the Prince of Troy really was, then Troy would have known to be ready for the Greek army. The situation also occurred in a time, where demands were made. It was about honor to make a demand for a return of a Greek citizen before waging war.

Men had to think about strategy and whether the war could be won, no matter the reason it might have started. Based on this knowledge, it is almost 100% certain the Trojans knew the Greeks were on their way to wage another battle before they arrived on the shores.

The best place for any ships to land was also in the protected harbor, which consistently gained shipping traffic when the winds did not support travel. To moor a ship in other areas would have been difficult, if not near to impossible, and it could have cost the Greek their ships.

It was not as if building a Greek warship could happen overnight or even within a few weeks. It took time to get the wood, mill the wood, and form it into the shape of a ship.

Some accounts believe Trojans would meet the Greeks on the field of battle, spar and then return to their fortress, while the Greeks would go back to their ships. It is a possibility. There were plenty of fields outside of the city walls that could have been used for battles.

If you assess Homer's written work, along with movies like Troy that try to depict the epic battle based on what is known of history, then it is possible a gentlemanly series of wars occurred.

Trojan men could have marched out of the city gates, stood strong and stopped the Greeks from getting inside the city. Trojans could also have stood on the fortress walls, lobbed fire balls, arrows, and hot oil down on the Greeks who were trying to batter their way into the citadel and the city.

Again, it is hard to say with any accuracy and in specific detail, regarding how the war was fought. All that can be said is what is in the books. Homer believed Trojans met on the field of battle, fought, died and kept the Greeks at bay each time.

The Greeks when readying for the war, would have brought some supplies, but not enough to last ten years. Supply ships might have been granted access during times of stalemates or agreed upon rests. Men could not fight day and night, continuously.

If there were even enough men to have several reserve fighters, it would have been difficult to try and battle in the dark hours. In fact, it would be foolhardy of either the Greeks or Trojans to have fought at night.

The armor was not the most comfortable or easiest to move in. Seeing by fire and moon did not mean success would occur. It was generally thought that war should be conducted with honor and strategy.

Surprise attacks such as leading the opposition into a trap was fine, but each needed time to pick up their wounded, their dead, and to pay proper respect to those who had fallen.

Whether the Greeks would return home each time, a battle was waged and lost, is not clear. According to Homer, they stayed near Troy and on Trojan fields. Homer also insists the battles occurred on fields that were often heavy with water, which would have made fighting difficult if not impossible for both parties.

Chapter 8:
Troy was Safe—At Least in Appearances

After what was ten or more years of consistent wars, it seemed like the Greeks had left, at least according to poetical accounts. Homer writes about the Greek ships leaving the harbor after one last battle, apparently knowing they were defeated, and that Troy could not be breached.

Homer also wrote of a present left behind. A relic, icon, or gift for the Trojans, thought to be a sign of peace. Finally, it seemed the Greeks would leave, allow Helen to remain with Paris, and alas peace would return for however long it might last.

Of course, this may not be how it happened at all. The reason many historians tend to agree with Homer's accounting comes down to the Trojan horse. Before getting too comfortable with the topic about the Trojan horse, which is ultimately the discussion to be had as a conclusion regarding the war, it is best to consider whether or not the Trojans would have brought a gift inside the gates of the citadel if the Greeks were still around.

If given a gift, it is natural to assume you would take it. You would not want to insult the person giving the gift and if a ten-year long war occurred, you might be inclined to think the opponent was finally out of strategies or men to continue with the war.

Still, you would be hesitant to accept a gift, particularly, if the entirety of the Greek army was still outside your walls. It would seem more likely in that scenario that the Greeks were waiting for you to fall for the gift, open the doors, and then attack.

The Trojan horse is considered a perfect strategy for sacking a city with few men because it was left as a present and the Greeks retreated. It would be easy for a leader, one tired of war, to think everything was finally over.

It is definitely the greatest strategy in history that the Greeks left and the Trojans fell for such a trick. Being lulled into a false sense of an end to any battle, whether it was the last in a long line of intermittent skirmishes or ten years of fighting, was most definitely the downfall of Troy.

Debating if the Greek Army Actually Left

There are historians who believe the Greek army did not leave. Instead, using something like a battering ram, rather than a Trojan horse, these scholars believe the Greeks finally made it through the gates of the city.

It is a likely scenario, just as likely, in fact, as a Trojan horse being built and left on Troy's doorstep. With continued breaks to recover from various skirmishes, the Greeks could have gone home several times to plan their next attack.

Animals in cages, who are unhappy to be there, will test every inch of their cage to determine any weak points. If a weak point is found after these tests, the animal will use it to escape. The Greeks could have tested and tested for more than ten years to find the weakest point in Troy's fortress, broken through, and sacked the city.

It is difficult to know since the city walls are mostly gone. All that remain of the Troy VIIa that was said to exist during the Trojan War, are ruins. Like many of the historical records for this time in history, there is little evidence to back up the epic poem Homer created. But what a tale of glory, he wrote.

A city that felt safe, a present filled with Greeks, and the end of a civilization.

Chapter 9:
Is the Trojan Horse Real?

A recent special series on the Trojan War and the horse that ended the war has provided new evidence to the academic world. Archeologists still digging around the city of Troy uncovered what they are calling the real Trojan horse.

These archeologists say they have uncovered several petrified wood pieces that make up the Trojan horse. The curve of the wood, the holes for the nails, and the total number of pieces uncovered are said to form what we have come to think of as the Trojan horse.

It is hard to argue with picture documentation, a PBS special, and archeologists who have worked extremely hard to uncover evidence regarding the Trojan War and the famed horse.

The academic community can; therefore, agree, Troy was not as safe as the Trojans must have thought. The Greeks did, in fact, present a gift filled with Greek soldiers.

But how did the Greek soldiers build such a gift, quickly, and without the Trojans being wary of such a build? Going back to Homer, it is said they built it all in one night using materials from a few of the Greek ships.

It is hard to agree that it would have been built in one night. Building the Trojan horse from boat material is certainly believable. It would have been all they had. If a ship had been destroyed during one of the battles, it is easy to assume it was reassembled into the "gift."

With many Greeks perishing in the war or various battles, it is also likely that the Greek warriors could have used the ships without worrying about the passengers. Less people going home alive would mean less ships could be brought home, after all, the warriors were also the power behind the ship's ability to move.

Before the planks were uncovered inside the citadel, several theories of what the Trojan horse actually was, were posed. Some thought the ships were made with removable pieces that were big enough to hold men, and with a little change in shape they put a horse head and legs on this part of the ship.

Other scholars thought it was nothing but a battering ram, given a special name as such things were in these times. These same scholars thought Homer was mistaken about what the phrase "Trojan horse" meant, so naturally he drew a giant horse, with men inside to depict the coup.

A structure that made legends, the Trojan horse is extremely important to the end of the Trojan civilization. The fact that evidence suggests it is real and was more of a horse shape, with men hiding inside, continues to hold our interest. There has even been some suggestion that the Greeks first thought of building a mallard, so instead of the Trojan horse it would have been the Trojan duck that rolled into the city of Troy and created such an infamous end to an epic battle. This little anecdote is just to show you that no matter what was used, a battering ram, a wooden horse, or a duck—the strategy of the Greeks was brilliant.

It has also helped shape many wars since, but let us not go into that concept yet.

Chapter 10:
The Stealthy Greeks

Inside the Trojan horse were ten brave men, according to Homer. Perhaps, there were more, maybe less. The important element is the strategy. Try as they might for ten years or several decades, the Greeks could not get into the city of Troy and put an end to the Trojan king and his people. Since the earthquake and subsequent rebuild, until sometime around 1180, Troy continued to prosper; Trojans continued to fight battles and win.

It was a time, when the Greeks had to develop a winning strategy or go home defeated yet again. They would have to continue to fear the Trojans would someday take a trip across the Dardanelles in their own warships and attempt to take over Greece.

The Mycenaean Greeks were suffering their own demise and collapse. Pylos was destroyed. More and more people were leaving the main cities due to natural disasters, maybe an illness, and certainly a desire to move on.

The historical accounts show the Mycenaean Greek civilizations, as they were known in the 1300s B.C., were losing the power they had. If something didn't change, they would be at the end of their civilization instead of the Trojans.

With plenty of battles fought and tests on the fortress walls of Troy, it is natural to assume, the Greeks had tried strategy after strategy, until finally coming up with one that will always amaze new civilizations.

We might not understand what the Trojan horse was, although evidence suggests it is exactly as Homer described, but we do know the Greeks were finally stealthy enough to trick the Trojans into letting them into the city.

The unburied skeletons found in the city do exist. There is always the argument that the Mycenaean Greek arrowheads were not related to those skeletons lying in the city streets; however, it seems likely from the oral accounts, poems, and the real Trojan horse that they did enter the city.

It would have been the perfect way for the Greeks to win the war. The Trojans, unsuspecting for the most part, certainly rolled the present into the citadel and were surprised enough by the sudden appearance of Greek warriors to be killed.

What came next is pure conjecture. Had the Trojans simply rolled the present in, leave it unattended save for a few warriors and go about their day? Is it possible that they were partying since the Greeks were gone? They might simply have been enjoying a meal when the Greeks made their way out of the horse for their surprise attack.

It would make sense that most of the Trojan warriors were not around the gift. Perhaps a few were guarding it to ensure nothing untold happened and they were overpowered by the Greeks coming out of the horse.

It seems highly likely that after any guards were killed that the Greeks would open the door to their fellow warriors. It would make more sense for the entire Greek army that was in the vicinity to have sailed back in the night, moored at the docks, made their way to the closed fortress gates, and helped sack the city.

Warfare at the time was nothing like it is now, in terms of the weapons or technology. Seeing at night would have been difficult. Killing with anything other than fire, swords, and arrows were less likely, certainly guns did not exist then. The more warriors let into the city, the easier it would be to suddenly end the fight.

The theory that if you kill the leader and all opposition stops is not truly how a war would end, even then. Battles at this time were about chivalry. It was one on one combat, bows and arrows, and sword fights. At the end of the day, the war was placed on hold for the wounded to be attended and men to prepare for the next battle.

Trojans would have been angered over the coup and certainly upset at the humiliation the deception caused. It was also a time when slaves were taken. Any surviving Trojans may well have been taken captive and made to work for the Greeks.

Since we cannot picture the entire battle, and can only assume what happened, it is up to you to decide if the entire Greek army entered the city that night. From a military standpoint, it makes sense for the Greeks to wait in a place on their ships that the Trojans would not be able to see. It also makes sense that their ships would have continued traveling back to Greece for a short time, until darkness fell and then for the Greeks to turn their ships back around in time for a predetermined time to meet their fellow warriors inside the city.

The element that is most important regarding the deception, is in truth the deception rather than what happened once the horse was inside. Certainly, if the coup had failed and the Greeks died inside the horse, the strategy and deception that became a part of later wars may not have happened in exactly the same way.

It is because the plan worked that history was forever changed in how to fight battles. Chivalry, heroes, and the gentlemanly fights on the battle fields that always ended for supper time didn't immediately change. But certain things did.

Chapter 11:
Getting into the City was the Battle

It is clear that forces attempted to get into Troy and destroy the middlemen. The Trojans were a civilization to fear only because they owned land that protected the coastal region for the Hittite Kingdom. The Hittites had plenty of enemies and they were Trojan allies.

Piecing together historical records and accounts, it is clear that war was a constant part of life. It is also clear that Troy or a city of a different name, was rebuilt time and again on the site, known as Hissarlik, in some of the texts.

Any of the known accounts of the time between 1300 B.C. and 1000 B.C. make it clear that Troy was a fortress that was hard to get into. One event is clearly considered the Trojan War, where the enemy attacked and the city was destroyed. Other endings to the cities built on that same site occurred due to natural disasters. It needs to be mentioned again that some destruction that occurred is unknown at this point.

The point in all of these statements—is the Greek army needed to get into the city. Homer and all other information says it was extremely difficult for the Greeks to breach the fortress walls and get into the city. These same accounts make it seem impossible for the Greeks to reach the king of Troy and put an end to him.

It could be debated all day and for centuries, and it certainly has that the reason the Greeks were so interested in Troy was their alliance with the Hittites and the location of this trade city to protecting the Hittite Kingdom.

An important factor is that the Greeks came up with the Trojan horse as a way to finally get into the city. More than half the battle, the Greeks faced was in ensuring they got through the tough walls and could reach the Trojan warriors to end them completely.

The Trojan horse is just the vessel that made this happen. No matter what tool was used, the fact that it worked, is how the course of history was changed for the Trojans.

The battle was pretty much over once the Greeks entered the city. It would have been difficult for the Trojan warriors to win, unless they were smart enough to wait for the surprise attack. We know the Trojans were caught by surprise, killed, and the city destroyed, thus they were not smart enough to see through the attack allowing the battle to be won as soon as they rolled the horse into their city.

Yes, obviously, there was still fighting that needed to occur. The Trojan warriors had to die or at least be submissive and accept the defeat. However, without the Trojan horse allowing entry into the city this would not have been the case.

It would be like someone consistently knocking on the door, asking for entry, and rebuffed time and again. Consider for a moment the ploys used by some famous serial killers, who killed their victims in their homes. These victims were lured by a ploy, one that seemed innocent and not harmful at all. In walks the intruder and death is a result.

Yet, if the victim denied entry, called the police, and remained safe inside where the killer could not get to them, their life would not have ended. In this context, it makes it clear that had the Trojans not allowed the Greeks in under the guise of a gift, the city might have lasted for a few more years, several more decades, or become an even greater power.

We might say the same thing of the Trojans. The Trojans unaware of the dangers lurking in the belly of a horse, let in the opposition and it was the end of the battle. All the Greeks had to do was find all the warriors, fight, wound or kill, and the city was theirs.

Chapter 12:
A Horse of a Different Color

Sorry for the play on words in the chapter title, but it was hard to resist. The Trojan War or series of wars could have ended much differently for the Trojans. Even according to Homer, had the Trojans followed the advice of certain characters, the coup would not have worked.

A strategy that we take as very simple in today's time, was magnificent in its simplicity to the point that it actually worked. It was unheard of for any real strategy to be a part of the battles waged during the Bronze Age. It was more about men going out, finding an opponent and seeing who might be killed or at least wounded. It was about making sure opponents could not return to the battlefield, more than deception and strategy.

If strategic warfare had been more common, then the horse that ended the Trojans in approximately 1180 B.C. may never have been an issue. Yes, Homer is fiction and a mythic, epic poem, but there is every chance some leader, warrior, or part of the royal party would have said burn the horse and don't you "dare bringing it inside the gates."

How would history be different if the horse never made it into the city of Troy? What if the Trojans were smart enough to recognize that the Greeks were trying one last ploy before really returning home, defeated?

For one thing, we would not be some enamored of the Trojan horse as a tool in the war. It might have taken well beyond the 5th century B.C. for similar deception strategies and strategic warfare to be considered. Then again, things might have happened the same way, only with one key difference. The Trojans would have been the winners of that battle instead of the Greeks.

It is easy to imagine that the Trojans would have been raising their weapons and cups in joy to show they did not fall for the ploy and then turn around and try to come up with a better strategy had they not seen their demise.

The Trojans could have very easily burned the horse and all of the Greeks inside. What made them bring the horse into the city instead?

For one, it could have been the way the war was waged at the time. Another reason is pride. The Greek ships were gone. They left a present as a peace offering, or so it appeared. Cheering that the war was over and the Greeks were beaten would have been easier than to worry about possible traps.

What if the Trojans had survived that skirmish? By all accounts, Troy was rebuilt a few more times, even with the fall of the "Greatest" Trojans. It could be argued that the fate of the Trojans was to die out, whether it happened in 1180 B.C. or in 500 A.D.

Another possible earthquake and attack did in another city, built on top of Troy. An unknown caused ended it a few times, so what or who is to say that Troy wouldn't have ended by another opponent in a similar way?

It is impossible to rewrite history. The Trojans of Homer's imagination scattered or died when the city was sacked by the Mycenaean Greeks. The Mycenaean Greeks didn't survive much longer either. In the end, other civilizations have started and stopped.

Today, people live in Turkey. The once grand city of Troy is a 75-acre dig site being excavated for knowledge, and we have air travel for better trade. Civilizations will continue to come and go. Advancements in human knowledge, technology, and various industries will continue.

But there is one thing that will remain a part of history forever—The Trojan horse and its meaning to later warfare. It is not a matter of whether the Trojan War occurred in ten years or a hundred. It is not that the Greeks won, it is how they won by using deception and a "horse" that make the history of the Trojans and Greeks important enough to write and read about.

Chapter 13:
The Impact the Trojan Horse Created

Homer took the information he learned about the Trojan War and wrote two epic poems. Historians cannot even agree on when he lived. Some believe he was born sometime in 1200 B.C. Others feel it is more likely that he was alive sometime in the 8th century B.C. For the most part the consensus is that Homer lived at least 400 years after the Trojan War took place.

Dating the poems is based on certain things mentioned about historical events that took place. Many believe Homer used wars prior to the Trojan War and after to create his tale. Homer was also not mentioned until around the 8th Century B.C. in historical texts.

The point is—the Trojan horse had an impact even after Troy VIIa fell because of the Greeks' deception. Without a written account that would interest listeners and readers, the Trojan horse might have fallen away into history, never to be known.

It is due to the Iliad and Odyssey, as well as other works that transcended time that numerous civilizations are aware of the Trojan War, the use of the Trojan horse, and the end of a once great city.

In the 5th century B.C., Sun Tzu wrote *The Art of War*. It became *the* military strategy guide for strategic warfare. The precepts he wrote about helped Asian armies fight amazing wars. But one has to ask, would Sun Tzu have come up with some of these concepts without the Trojan horse? Maybe, it would take a deeper look into how far the Iliad and other Trojan War stories travelled, but the fact remains the Trojan horse had a significant impact on how wars were fought in Asia Minor and later on.

Even today, the simplicity of the Trojan horse is considered in certain circumstances, albeit a different version, but nevertheless similar concepts are used. If you think about it, military personnel going in during the night to try and capture an enemy, dates back to the time when the Trojan horse was used.

Archeological Impact

It is not just about the way war might have changed and did change after the tale of the Trojan horse made its way around the world—it is also archeology. Numerous archeologists have spent countless hours searching for and digging up Troy. These many people dug and dug until they found Troy VIIa. These same archeologists have worked to find corresponding texts, written and oral evidence, and artifacts that can confirm the Trojan war happened and the Trojan horse was as glorious an end to the Trojan civilization as Homer made it out to be.

We are still trying to determine the truth of the war. Many still create pictures and TV shows to share their theory of what happened, as well as the evidence to back it up. Historical writers read through various material, visit the site, and attempt to discuss the Trojan War and how the Trojan horse ended a ten-year or longer battle.

The Trojan horse as a war strategy interests us. We can't help, but try to find the answers. Simply put, the war happened either due to a woman or due to the location of Troy and the fear the Greeks felt.

The war was fought as any war during that time, until one or more intelligent Mycenaean Greek warriors came up with the strategy to use the Trojan horse to completely annihilate the Trojans.

Chapter 14:
The Trojans Lived, Weakened Perhaps

Homer made it sound like the heroes who helped the Greek, made their way home and the Trojans were a forgotten people. We know that Troy rose again. It was not just a city of Greeks once it was rebuilt. Perhaps the Greeks gave up wanting the city or maybe they couldn't hold onto it as their own demise began in earnest.

Those who lived in Troy VIIb1 through VIIb3, could well have been descendants of the Trojans who perished in the Trojan War. It is clear that some part of their DNA remains given the Etruscan connection.

While Homer's Trojans were completely annihilated and wiped off the map, the real truth is a part of them still live on in the descendants that remain, even if the blood is diluted numerous times over.

Like the Romans, who rose to power later on, it is possible that the Trojan warriors were kept as slaves, at least those who did not die in the war. It is also possible that the woman of Troy became wives to Greek husbands, and continued a nomadic existence as the Mycenaean Greeks fell from power and started moving to refugee locations.

Others most likely returned to the city they knew after it was clear the Greeks or whoever rebuilt the city would not kill them on sight.

A lesson that can be learned here is that while wars are fought in the moment of history, when it ends and when a civilization ends or changes into a new group, a war waged may no longer be of importance for millennia.

Look at how long it took for us to uncover the truth about the Trojan War. It was not until 145 years ago we took the Trojan War as true history. The Trojan horse was considered a fictional concept until the planks of what are most likely the Trojan remains were found.

Only the lesson that allowing a gift passed your fortress walls, the gate to your home, or through your front door is what is really most important. Without that lesson things might have been different. We might not remember to be careful, when a stranger approaches. It is very possible that we may never have considered the dangers of a mundane object as dangerous, at least not in the context that we do today.

So the Trojans live, whether in our DNA or because of the lesson their error has taught us. In one day, when the Trojans found the horse, their lives as they knew them ended and the Trojan War or various wars ended for at least a little while, until the city was built again.

Conclusion

Thank you for purchasing this book!

I hope this book was able to help you understand the historical aspects of the Trojan War, the part the Trojan horse played in that war, and how the demise of a society occurred.

Hopefully, you found a little pleasure in reading about these long ago times, with these long ago warriors who may have fought over a woman or simply wanted to protect what they felt was important.

The Trojan horse, whether real or of Homer's imagination, has definitely left an impact on the world, including one on today's world. An innovative concept that a war could be won with a gift of hidden soldiers is and always will be considered one of the greatest feats of history. Certainly the strategy and intelligence behind such a concept is one that makes you reconsider all war strategies.

Finally, if you enjoyed this book, please take the time to share your thoughts and post a review on Amazon. It would be greatly appreciated!

Thank you and good luck!

Preview of Greek Gods by Patrick Auerbach

Introduction

Greek mythology is deeply ingrained in our culture. References to it are everywhere. In psychology we have the Oedipus complex and the opposition of Apollonian and Dionysian temperaments. In popular speech we describe epic journeys as odysseys, speak of other people 'opening Pandora's box' or 'having the golden touch,' and describe certain types of computer malware as 'Trojan horses.' Western literature and drama, of course, owe a deep debt to the Greek myths. Eugene O'Neill's Mourning Becomes Electra and Sartre's The Flies are two very different reinterpretations of the story of Orestes and Electra. Paul Frazer's Civil War novel Cold Mountain draws heavily on the Odyssey. Cocteau's Orphee, Rilke's Sonnets to Orpheus and Tennessee Williams' Orpheus Descending are all drawn from the same myth cycle.

It's difficult to draw up one comprehensive account of Greek mythology. Greek creation stories and accounts of the gods are many, varied and contradictory. Cultural understandings and religious practices changed, and the sacred stories shifted with them. When the Roman empire conquered the Greek lands they took over the Greek pantheon, renamed all the deities, and added in some stories of their own. What follows is an introduction to some of the common understandings of the gods and to some of the great cosmic and human stories that have left an enduring mark on our culture. Further reading suggestions are in the 'Sources' section at the end.

Chapter One:
The Creation and the Gods

In The Beginning...

How did the world begin? The stories vary widely. One common feature is that the gods who reigned on Mount Olympus, the gods featured in the legends and the worship of the time, were the world's children, not its creators. In the beginning was chaos. From this chaos the first divine beings arose, and from their couplings life and order filled the void. But there was still plenty of chaos to go around. The ancient gods made war on each other, and there was great destruction before the Olympian gods arose and the world gained a precarious stability. Even the Olympians were hardly of one mind, and the wars of men were complicated, sometimes determined, by the power-struggles of the gods.

The Olympian creation myth, which was at some point the canonical version, says that in the beginning Gaia, the Earth, emerged from Chaos and, in her sleep, bore a son, Uranus, who ascended to the mountaintops and showered her with fertile rain; she conceived and bore other children--plants, beasts, birds, fish, one-eyed Cyclopes, hundred-handed Hecatoncheires, and also the Titans, the vast and powerful ancestors of the Olympian gods.

Uranus, wishing to maintain control of the world, imprisoned the Cyclopes and Hecatoncheires in the dark depths of Tartarus, far below the earth. Gaia was furious and encouraged the Titans, who were still free, to attack Uranus. Cronus, the boldest of them, did so, castrating him. Uranus either died or fled, predicting that Cronus also would be overthrown by his children. The splashing foam produced by

Uranus' genitals and Cronus' sickle falling into the sea engendered Aphrodite (Venus to the Romans), the goddess of love; Uranus' blood falling on the land brought forth the nymphs, the giants, and also the Furies, who punish mortals who kill or injure their relatives.

Cronus, victorious, did not release the prisoners from Tartarus. He married his sister Rhea and set himself up as ruler of the world. To prevent Uranus' prophecy from coming true he swallowed all the children Rhea bore him; but when she bore Zeus she gave the child to Gaia to hide, and gave her husband a stone to swallow. Zeus was raised in secret. As he grew to maturity he asked the Titaness Metis to help him defeat his father and revive his siblings. Metis gave Cronus a potion that made him vomit forth his children, who promptly joined Zeus in making war on the Titans. After a ten-year struggle, Gaia urged Zeus to free the Cyclopes and Hecatoncheires, who would prove formidable allies; Zeus did so, and they armed him with the thunderbolt, also giving powerful weapons to his brother gods. Cronus and the other male Titans were then banished to Tartarus, promising that Zeus also would be overthrown by one of his sons. Atlas, who had led the Titans in war, was punished by being forced to hold up the world. Metis and the Titanesses remained free, as did the Titans Prometheus and Epimetheus, who had taken joined with the Olympians before the end.

The Olympian Gods (and a few others)

The Olympian gods, and the Titans who were left to rule with them, were the great supernatural figures in the foreground of the myths. However, they were not all-powerful. Their destinies as well as those of mortals were determined by the Moirae or Fates, three women who worked together on a tapestry whose threads were the lives of all living things. Their ancestry was unknown and their workings were mysterious, even to the gods.

Gods:

Zeus (called Jupiter or Jove by the Romans) was the greatest of the Olympian gods, ruler of the skies and wielder of the thunderbolt. His power was great but not infinite, and he could be deceived. He could also be deceitful--though married to Hera, he had frequent affairs with attractive goddesses, nymphs and mortal women, which he tried (usually unsuccessfully) to conceal from his wife. He expected righteous behavior from humans--oath-keeping, respect for the dead, and kindness to beggars and strangers.

Poseidon (Neptune to the Romans), brother of Zeus, was second greatest of the gods, the ruler of the sea, creator of horses, and wielder of an immensely powerful trident made for him by the Cyclopes.

Hades, (Pluto to the Romans), brother of Zeus, was the ruler of the underworld (named Hades after him) and the dead. He had a helmet of invisibility given to him by the Cyclopes.

Apollo, son of Zeus and the Titan Leto, twin brother of Artemis, was the god of the sun, the arts, and prophecy. He could not lie. His oracle at Delphi gave true answers to every question, although sometimes the truth was stated so mysteriously that the questioner went home no wiser. He also gave the gift of prophecy to Cassandra, a mortal woman, princess of Troy, when he was courting her; when she refused him, he couldn't take the gift back, but he added the curse that her prophecies would never be believed. Apollo was also the protector of herdsmen and shepherds and the father of Asclepius, the god of healing.

Dionysus (Bacchus to the Romans), son of Zeus and either Demeter or Semele depending on which myth you read, was the god of wine, fertility, ecstasy, madness, and the theater. His death and rebirth are associated with the changes of the seasons. He gave grapes to humans and taught the art of wine-making. Dionysus sometimes granted dangerous wishes to mortals. He offered King Midas anything he wanted, and Midas asked to have everything he touched turn to gold. Dionysus granted the wish and watched while the king's food and drink turned to gold as he touched them, while his dearly loved daughter went to comfort him and turned to gold as she embraced him. Then Dionysus had pity on the king, restored the girl to life and and took the gift back.

Eros (Cupid to the Romans) was the god of love and desire. In some stories he is one of the first gods to arise from chaos; in others he is the son of Aphrodite, by either her husband Hephaestus or her lover Ares. Eros' arrows, often shot at random, caused mortals and immortals who were struck by them to fall in love. Eros himself fell in love with Psyche; their story is told below.

Ares (Mars to the Romans), son of Zeus and Hera, was the god of war in general (as opposed to defensive war, Athena's specialty). Many of the Greeks looked down on him as bloodthirsty and mindless; many of the Romans looked up to him as valiant and glorious.

Hermes (Mercury to the Romans), whose father was Zeus and whose mother was Atlas' daughter Maia, was the god of thieves and of commerce; as a day-old child he stole Apollo's cattle and, when Apollo came to reclaim them, got Apollo to leave them with him in exchange for the lyre, which he had just invented and was willing to trade away. Hermes also carried messages for Zeus and guided souls to the world of the dead. Pan, the god of shepherds, was Hermes' son.

Hephaestus (Vulcan to the Romans), son of Hera--some say hers only, some say hers by Zeus--was the smith to the gods, maker of their weapons and also of the lovely things which adorn Mount Olympus. He was crippled, having been thrown down from Olympus either by Hera (who was disappointed by his ugliness) or by Zeus (who was angry with him for standing up for his mother); but after his fall he was loved and honored by the Olympians. He was also honored by humans, to whom he taught metalwork and other necessary crafts. He was a gentle and peace-loving god. In many stories he was married to Aphrodite, though she was enamored of Ares and had an affair with him.

Prometheus was one of the Titans who survived into the age of the Olympian gods. In some stories he helped Athena to emerge from the head of Zeus. He was the maker and protector of humanity, at great cost to himself; he became the god of science. More of his story is told in "Prometheus, Epimetheus and Pandora" below.

Goddesses:

Hera, (Juno to the Romans), wife and sister of Zeus, was the protector of married women and mothers. Most of the stories about her describe her jealousy of Zeus and her revenges on his paramours.

Athena (Minerva to the Romans), who sprang full-fledged from the head of Zeus rather than being born in the usual way, was the goddess of wisdom and of defensive war (in most accounts--though in the Iliad she's described as being on the side of the Greek attackers of Troy.). Poseidon created horses, but Athena tamed them. She taught mortals to plow and raise crops and tame animals, she created the first olive tree, and she invented pottery, weaving and spinning. She could also be vindictive. When a mortal woman named Arachne claimed that she could weave as well as Athena, and actually challenged her to a weaving contest where she wove as skillfully as Athena (showing scenes of the Gods behaving foolishly, whereas Athena's tapestry showed the Gods in their glory), Athena destroyed Arachne's web and struck her with fear and shame so that she hanged herself. Athena pitied her then and brought her back to life as a spider. Our word 'arachnid' comes from Arachne's name.

Aphrodite (Venus to the Romans), born of the foam of the sea, was the goddess of love, supremely beautiful and the giver of joy. She could also be cruel, deceiving men and driving them to despair. In most myths her husband is Hephaestus and her lover is Ares.

Artemis (Diana to the Romans), daughter of Zeus and Leto and twin sister of Apollo, was the virgin goddess of the hunt, wilderness and wild creatures, virginity, childbirth and children. In later stories she is said to be the same as Selene, goddess of the moon, and Hecate, goddess of the underworld.

Demeter (Ceres to the Romans), sister of Zeus, was the goddess of the harvest and the earth's fertility. Athena taught men to plow, but Demeter gave them grain, and Demeter caused all growth. Demeter's beautiful daughter, Persephone (Proserpina to the Romans), was abducted by Hades; Demeter, who hadn't seen what happened, searched for her for a long time, grieving, and her grief stopped life and growth. Zeus, wishing the world to live, ordered Hades to send

Persephone back; but Persephone had eaten in the Underworld and could not leave it forever. For four months of the year she was bound to return to Hades, and once again Demeter grieved and growth was halted, but for the remainder of the year Persephone was with her mother and all green things grew and thrived. According to some stories Dionysus is Demeter's son.

Hestia (Vesta to the Romans), sister of Zeus, was the virgin goddess of home and hearth.

Click here to check out the rest of Greek Gods on Amazon.com

Or go to: **Amazon UK Link** (if you live in the United Kingdom)

Made in the USA
Middletown, DE
23 March 2017